FAITH from My Own Perspective

FRUITFULNESS|ASSEMBLING|INPIRING|TRUTHFULNESS|HAPPINESS

To my wife Tsembekile Nthabiseng Mkhonta and our daughter Thubalenkosi Abigail Mkhonta, you are my inspiration.

Bonginkosi Siyabonga Mkhonta

Preface

According to the English Oxford Living Dictionaries, there are two meanings of FAITH:

a) A complete trust or confidence in someone or something. 'This restores one's faith in politicians'.

b) A strong belief in the doctrine of a religion, based on spiritual conviction rather than proof. 'Bereaved people who have shown supreme faith'.

In Christianity, faith is defined differently when compared to the English Oxford Living Dictionaries. The Bible states clearly, in Hebrews 11: 1 NKJV that "Now faith is the substance of things hoped for, the evidence of things not seen".

I was inspired to write this book, based on my personal experiences of faith, about what God has done for me, is doing for me and what He will do for me. As a Christian I've always believed and had faith in Jesus Christ and God Almighty. I hope this book will inspire and encourage other Christians' faith to grow through Christ Jesus, or non-believers to turn to God and receive Jesus Christ as their Lord and Saviour.

The word FAITH in this book is broken down into five concepts: (**F**ruitfulness, **A**ssembling, **I**nspirational, **T**ruthful and **H**appiness) and I will be discussing these in the next chapters, with references based on the Bible and my life experiences.

I received Christ Jesus as my Lord and saviour when I was young in Sunday school but I was baptized when I was nineteen years old, on the 4th of September 2005. This was the best decision I ever made, not because I was doing wrong things per se, but because as a Christian I must be born again.

The Bible states, in Romans 5:12, that "Therefore, just as through one man sin entered the world and death through sin, and thus death spread to all men, because all sinned".

I have come across great men and women of faith in my life who influenced me in a positive way and helped me to grow in my faith. To mention only a few, and not in any particular order, some of these are: Bishop Tshalo Katshunga, Bishop Absalom M. Mnisi, Mr. Rocky Mabaso, Sibonakaliso A. Vilakati, Ms. Dum'sile Malambe, Fr. Martin McCormack, my wife Tsembekile Mkhonta, Mxolisi Nyaweni, Mama Beatrice Katshunga, Innocentia Mboweni, Pastor David T. Ndlela,

Mama Sanna P. Mnisi, Steve Biruli Asan, Henry B. Murphy, Tatenda Zingoni, Constance Zingoni, gran Esther N. Dlamini, Mr. Douglas V. Vilakati, Mrs. Glory N. Vilakati, Alan Johnstone, all my family members and friends.

There are many others I owe my gratitude to but who are not mentioned because of space and time.

Notable Christian faith quotes:

a) I believe that, if you keep your faith, you keep your trust, you keep the right attitude, if you're grateful, you'll see God open doors. – Joel Osteen

b) Be faithful in small things because it is in them that your strength lies. – Mother Teresa

c) Faith is taking the first step, even if you don't see the staircase.–Martin Luther King, Jr.

d) God will never give you anything you can't handle, so don't stress. – Kelly Clarkson

e) The foundation stones for a balanced success are honesty, character, integrity, faith, love and loyalty. – Zig Ziglar

FRUITFULNESS: CHAPTER 1

My dream

First and foremost, in order to be positively influential in your Christian life and faith, you must be *fruitful*. I can remember as vividly as if it was yesterday that it was the wee hours of the morning on the 1st of January 2019. I had a rather concerning dream. In my dream I saw two ladies, mother and daughter. They were sleeping in a tent. The daughter had a son, about two years old, and the young boy looked me straight in my eyes and smiled.

I felt in my spirit to pray for them. The daughter had letters engraved on her back which read, "love you son" and a red heart stuck next to the words. I offered to pray for her because the words couldn't come off her back and she didn't know who'd put them there. She believed it was evil spirits, even though they appeared to mean no harm when you read them. She agreed to be prayed for. As soon as I said "Amen", the words fell off her back. I was also able to help them financially and I felt peace in my heart - and then I woke up.

After I woke up, nothing made sense at all to me about the dream. I thought I had been hallucinating and I remembered two great men in the Bible: Joseph and Daniel. I may not be Joseph or Daniel in the Bible, who could interpret dreams, but the dream made me realize five things:

a) Pray for people who are sick and they will be healed (faith).

b) Help others in order to grow financially and spiritually (generosity).

c) Have a good source of income in order to be God's kingdom financier (be a blessing).

d) Generosity and kindness will be your greatest tools to be fruitful (Galatians 6:9).

e) The devil disguises himself as a sheep in a wolf skin (be vigilant).

Let us discus the points above, linking them to scriptures in the Bible and their connection to being fruitful through faith, starting from the dream itself. The dreams reminded me of two great men of God in the Bible who were full of faith and were fruitful: Joseph and Daniel.

These men were in God's heart and they had to suffer first in order for God's power to be shown. They also saw visions and dreams which edified to the identification of the true God.

Joseph's dreams

NKJV Genesis 37:7 – There we were, binding sheaves in the field. Then behold, my sheaf arose and also stood upright; and indeed your sheaves stood all around and bowed down to my sheaf. NKJV Genesis 37:9 – Then he dreamed still another dream and told it to his brothers, and said, "Look, I have dreamed another dream. And this time, the sun, the moon, and the eleven stars bowed down to me."

We may be familiar with Joseph's story from Sunday school classes or some of the Bible teachings or sermons to be found on the internet. We can summarize Joseph's story in the following passage as per IMDb website Plot Summary (2) by Anonymous.

Joseph's story is found in the book of Genesis 37 – 50 in the Bible. The summary is based on the chapters mentioned above. "The story begins in Egypt, in the marketplace of Avaris, where Joseph is sold as a slave to Potiphar, the Pharaoh's Chief Steward.

Joseph, the favoured son of the patriarch Jacob, was given into captivity by his own envious brothers. A tireless and highly productive worker, Joseph wins his master's trust and is named steward of Potiphar's household. However, Joseph also unwittingly arouses the lust of Potiphar's wife.

Luring him into her room one day, she orders Joseph to give her pleasure. But Joseph prefers punishment, even death, to betraying his master. As he flees from the room, the desperate woman tears off Joseph's garment and brandishes it as proof of her violation.

As Potiphar questions him, Joseph begins to narrate the story of his past, a tale of suffering and hardship. We flash back to the time when Jacob and his family settled near the town of Schechem.

It is a brief and unhappy stay, for when Jacob's daughter Dinah is ravished by the young prince of Schechem, Jacob's sons decide to exact revenge with a bloodbath - despite an agreement reached between Jacob and the Schechemites. As Jacob and his family flee, Rachel, Jacob's beloved wife, dies while giving birth to Benjamin. A few years elapse, and Jacob's older sons become increasingly resentful of their father's preference for Joseph.

When Joseph turns seventeen, his father has a wonderful coloured coat made for him, which further excites the jealousy of the brothers. When Joseph is sent to a distant pasture one day to look for his brothers, they seize him, tear off his coat, throw him into a dry well and, the following day, sell him as a slave to traders on their way to Egypt. This is how he enters the service of Potiphar. Despite his doubts about his wife's version of the "rape", Potiphar has Joseph jailed to vindicate his wife publicly.

In prison, Joseph is assigned to attend two high court officials who are suspected of having stolen a bracelet from the Pharaoh. Tormented by dreams, the men ask Joseph for help. Joseph tells the cup-bearer that he will be reinstated and the chief-baker that he will hang. Two years later, the cup-bearer remembers Joseph when the Pharaoh is unable to obtain from his priests a rational interpretation of two anguishing dreams.

Joseph is summoned and predicts that after seven years of plentiful harvest, Egypt will suffer seven years of famine. Convinced, Pharaoh then appoints Joseph as his chancellor and gives him a beautiful Egyptian woman as his wife. Joseph immediately begins to put aside a fifth of the country's harvest. After seven years, a murderous famine strikes, driving people from nations near and far to come to Egypt to buy grain. Among the famished, Joseph recognizes his brothers.

Testing them to see if they have changed, Joseph is satisfied and reveals himself. Finally reunited with his beloved brother

Benjamin and his father Jacob, Joseph reconciles with his family, and the Pharaoh invites them to settle in Egypt as overseers of his livestock."

Source: https://m.imdb.com/title/tt0113483/plotsummary

How was Joseph fruitful?

a) NIV Genesis 49:22 says, "Joseph is a fruitful vine, a fruitful vine near a spring, whose branches climb over a wall." We can recall that these were Jacob's last words to his sons. He called them and told them what will befall them in the last days.
    If we read Genesis we see that he described all his sons one by one, but when he came to describe Joseph, he said "… is a fruitful vine near a spring" and that shows how important Joseph was not only to Jacob but to the nation of Israel as whole.

b) After Joseph was sold as a slave by his brothers, not only did he remain faithful to God despite his abandonment, but he also remained faithful to his family in forgiving them, rather than blaming them. Ultimately, his faithfulness led to great fruitfulness.

c) A lesson we can derive from Joseph's story of fruitfulness is that he remained calm and collected throughout all the trials and tribulations he faced.

    As Christians, it's important to remain focused on God throughout all tribulations because God will never leave us or forsake us. NIV Deuteronomy 31:6 says,

"Be strong and courageous. Do not be afraid or terrified because of them, for the LORD your God goes with you; He will never leave you nor forsake you."

d) Joseph was wrongfully accused of rape by Potiphar's wife and was sent to prison. God was with Joseph throughout his trials. ESV Matthew 5: 11 says, "Blessed are you when others revile you and persecute you and utter all kinds of evil against you falsely on my account." Joseph never tried to defend himself in any way, but he knew that he was innocent and he put all his trust in God. NKJV Genesis 39: 21 says, "But the Lord was with Joseph and showed him mercy, and He gave him favour in the sight of the keeper of the prison."

e) Joseph didn't take revenge against his brothers when he was a governor in Egypt. NKJV Genesis 42:6 says, "Now Joseph was governor over the land; and it was he who sold to all the people of the land. And Joseph's brothers came and bowed down before him with their faces to the earth."

Here we see a loving and forgiving Joseph. It's a sign of being fruitful. He could easily have avenged himself against his brothers who'd separated him from his family for so many years and caused him to have to live with strangers in a foreign land. ESV 1 Peter 3:9 says, "Do not repay evil for evil or reviling for reviling, but on the contrary, bless, for to this you were called, that you may obtain a blessing."

f) Joseph showed great faith in God. NKJV Genesis 50: 19
   – 20 says: Joseph said to them, "Do not be afraid, for am
   I not in the place of God? But as for you, you meant evil
   against me; but God meant it for good, in order to bring
   it about as it is this day, to save many people alive."
   From these verses we learn that Joseph understood that
   he had to go through these trials in order to triumph at
   the end of it all.

g) Indeed, the end is better than the beginning, it is better to
   start badly than to end badly and we can also derive from
   the scripture that Joseph had a godly mind-set.

Daniel's dream and vision

This passage will focus on Daniel's dreams as summarized on
www.gotquestions.org. At certain times, God has used dreams
to communicate with people. One of those people was King
Nebuchadnezzar of Babylon. Daniel 2 tells how Daniel
interpreted Nebuchadnezzar's dream, in which God provided an
overview of world events in the millennia yet to come.

Character Backgrounds: King Nebuchadnezzar reigned from
605 to 562 B.C., greatly expanding the Babylonian Empire,
conquering Jerusalem and deporting the Jews in the process.
Daniel was one of those deported from Israel and granted an
education in the king's palace. When God granted Daniel the
wisdom to interpret the king's dream, it launched Daniel's long
career as a political leader, trusted advisor and well-known
prophet.

Nebuchadnezzar's Nightmare

Nebuchadnezzar awoke frightened by a dream. The king called for his magicians to interpret the nightmare. This was standard procedure in a culture that placed high importance on dreams and their meaning. However, he added an unprecedented requirement: "Tell me what my dream was and interpret it" (Daniel 2:5).

So, not only did the royal wise men have to provide the interpretation of the dream, they had to recount the dream itself. The penalty for failure was death. Every magician, enchanter, sorcerer and astrologer in the kingdom would be executed.

The worried magicians replied, "What the king asks is too difficult. No one can reveal it to the king except the gods, and they do not live among men" (Daniel 2:11). When Daniel heard of this, he was determined to prove God's power to the king (Daniel 2:18).

Daniel's response: The Dream. Daniel asked the king for some time to discover the dream, and then he proceeded to pray all night with three of his fellow exiles. God revealed the dream to him, and Daniel and his friends praised God (Daniel 2:19-23).

The next morning, he went to the king and told him about the dream. The dream featured a huge, glorious statue of a man. Its head was made of pure gold, its chest and arms of silver, its belly and thighs of bronze, its legs of iron, its feet partly of iron and partly of baked clay (Daniel 2:32-33).

Then a rock, cut not by human hands (Daniel 2:34), hit the foot of the statue, and the whole image became like chaff on a threshing floor, while the rock became a huge mountain and filled the whole earth (Daniel 2:35). This vision, by the way, gives us our modern idiom "feet of clay", meaning "a hidden fault or weakness".

Daniel's response: The Interpretation. Daniel's interpretation, given to him by God, explains that the statue represents a series of kingdoms, each less glorious than the one before, as indicated by the decreasing value of the metals. Daniel identifies Nebuchadnezzar as the head of gold, stating that God had given Nebuchadnezzar much power (Daniel 2:37-38).

The next kingdom to arise would be inferior to Babylon, as would the next. Finally, there would come a fourth kingdom, strong as iron. It would crush and break all the others (Daniel 2:40). Finally, the feet of mixed clay and iron would be a divided kingdom (Daniel 2:41). During the time of this final world empire, the rock would smash them all to bits. This is a prediction that God will set up a kingdom that can never be destroyed (Daniel 2:44). All previous earthly kingdoms will be brought to an end.

Daniel's Dream 2,500+ Years Later

The first four kingdoms have been identified as the Babylonian, Persian, Greek and Roman Empires. This identification has come from the workings of history matching other prophecies. Daniel has already said that Babylon, specifically Nebuchadnezzar, was the head of gold (Daniel 2:38).

Babylon fell to the kingdom of the Medes and the Persians (Daniel 5:26-31). Greece became the successor to the Medo-Persian Empire (Daniel 8:20-21; 10:20 - 11:14). The iron empire can only be Rome.

Opinions differ on the fifth empire. Some have tried to identify various periods in Europe's history as the clay-and-iron feet; others claim the feet represent the divided remnants of Rome before supposedly being conquered by Christianity. Still others believe that the clay/iron empire is yet to come: the kingdom of the Antichrist will be a revived Roman Empire.

The last theory seems to be the best. We know, according to Revelation 17:12-13, that the Antichrist will lead a coalition of ten nations (the statue's ten toes?). And we know that Christ will defeat the forces of the Antichrist (Revelation 17:14). After that, Jesus will set up His kingdom—the rock smashes the image—and the kingdoms of this world will become the kingdom of our Lord and of His Christ, and He will reign for ever and ever (Revelation 11:15).

Many scholars have contrasted Nebuchadnezzar's dream in Daniel 2 with Daniel's vision in Chapter 7. Both passages reveal the coming world kingdoms, but the symbolism is strikingly different in each.

The pagan king sees the kingdoms of this world as a towering work of art, impressive in size, value and grandeur (albeit with feet of clay). God's prophet sees the same kingdoms as bizarre, unnatural beasts, terrifying in aspect and behaviour.

It's a difference of perspective: where man sees a stately, glittering tribute to himself, God sees a menagerie of aberrations. Let us not be desirous of vain glory (Galatians 5:26, KJV). Source: https://www.gotquestions.org/Nebuchadnezzars-dream.html

How was Daniel Fruitful?

a) God granted Daniel the wisdom to interpret the king's dream. It launched Daniel's long career as a political leader, trusted advisor and well-known prophet. Daniel used his wisdom for a good cause. He didn't use it to manipulate people or for his own benefit; hence we can conclude that he was indeed fruitful.

   James 3:17 says, "But the wisdom that comes from heaven is first of all pure; then peace-loving, considerate, submissive, full of mercy and good fruit, impartial and sincere."

b) Daniel was one of those deported from Israel and granted an education in the king's palace. From this sentence we can see that not only did Daniel have wisdom, but he was also educated in the king's palace. This, however, didn't go to Daniel's head. He remained humble.

   NAS 1977 Daniel 1:5 says, "And the king appointed them a daily ration from the king's choice food and from the wine which (the king) drank, and appointed that they should be educated three years, at the end of which they were to enter the king's personal service."

c) When Daniel heard of this, he was determined to prove God's power to the king. This sentence refers to when the king asked his magicians not only to provide the interpretation of the dream; they also had to recount the dream itself. The penalty for failure was death: every magician, enchanter, sorcerer and astrologer in the kingdom would be executed.

NIV Daniel 2:18 says, "He (Daniel) urged them (exile friends Hananiah, Amishael and Azariah) to plead for mercy from the God of heaven concerning this mystery, so that he and his friends might not be executed with the rest of the wise men of Babylon.

d) Then a rock, cut not by human hands (Daniel 2:34), hit the foot of the statue, and the whole image became like chaff on a threshing floor, while the rock became a huge mountain and filled the whole earth (Daniel 2:35).

In this context, the rock represents Jesus. Daniel was being fruitful, as he spoke about the rock (Jesus) way before Jesus was born, foretelling that Christ will defeat the forces of the antichrist (Revelation 17:14). After that, Jesus will set up His kingdom—the rock smashes the image—and the kingdoms of this world will become the kingdom of our Lord and of His Christ, and He will reign for ever and ever (Revelation 11:15).

The biblical meaning of fruitfulness

According to www.gotquestions.org, The Bible often uses the
metaphor of fruit to describe the product of our lives. Fruit can
be either good or bad (Matthew 7:18; Luke 6:43).

Romans 7:5 says, "For when we were in the realm of the flesh…
we bore fruit for death." A fruitful Christian will produce better
results: "The fruit of the righteous is a tree of life" (Proverbs
11:30).

Fruit is the direct result of whatever controls our hearts
(Matthew 15:19). The fruit of a life not surrendered to Jesus
includes sexual immorality, impurity and debauchery, idolatry
and witchcraft, hatred, discord, jealousy, fits of rage, and many
more evil acts (Galatians 5:19– 20). In contrast, the fruit of the
Spirit of God is love, joy, peace, patience, kindness, goodness,
faithfulness, gentleness, and self-control (Galatians 5:22–23).

God the Father is the Gardener (John 15:1), and He desires us to
be fruitful. Jesus said, "I am the vine; you are the branches. If
you remain in me and I in you, you will bear much fruit; apart
from me you can do nothing" (John 15:5). As branches cling to
the vine, we cling to Christ, drawing our very life from Him.
The goal is "much fruit", as Christ uses us to bring about
blessed, celestial results in a broken, fallen world.

When we have committed ourselves to Christ and live to please
Him, the natural result is behavioural choices that look like His.
He was clear that true followers of Christ will be recognizable
by their fruit. Do people pick grapes from thorn bushes, or figs
from thistles?

Likewise, every good tree bears good fruit, but a bad tree bears
bad fruit. A good tree cannot bear bad fruit, and a bad tree
cannot bear good fruit.

Every tree that does not bear good fruit is cut down and thrown
into the fire. Thus, by their fruit you will recognize them
(Matthew 7:16–20). There are many ways Christians can be
fruitful. True fruitfulness begins in the heart with the fruit of the
Spirit.

That inner fruit affects outward actions; our words and our
activities will glorify the Lord, and God's will is accomplished.
God's desire is to transform us into the image of Christ (Romans
8:29) and make us as fruitful as He was.

In our allegiance to Him, we want to be characterized by good
works (Ephesians 2:10; Titus 2:7; Colossians 1:10), humility
(Ephesians 4:2; Titus 3:2), and forgiveness (Ephesians 4:32;
Colossians 3:13). We want to always be ready to give an
account for the hope that is within you (1 Peter 3:15). We desire
to be the "good soil" Jesus spoke of in the Parable of the sower
in Matthew 13:3–9.

The result of spiritual fruitfulness is that God is glorified, we
grow, and others come to know Christ—this is the ultimate
fruitfulness for a child of God (Matthew 5:16; Acts 20:26–27;
Mark 16:15).

Source: https://www.gotquestions.org/fruitful-Christian.html

ASSEMBLING: CHAPTER 2

Secondly, to be positively influential in your Christian life and faith, you must *assemble* with other brethren in order to grow spiritually. When you come together to discuss and share the word of God, you grow in your Christian life. According to www.dictionary.com assembling has several meanings;

a) To bring together or gather or gather into one place, company, body, or whole.

b) To put or fit together; put together parts of.

c) To come together; gather; meet.

From the above meanings we can conclude that assembling is all about the coming together of people, things or parts. The Bible says, in Hebrews 10:24-25 NKJV, "And let us consider one another in order to stir up love and good works, not forsaking the assembling of ourselves together, as is the manner of some, but exhorting one another, and so much the more as you see the Day approaching."

When discussing assembling, one cannot ignore the work of the apostles. The beauty of their work can be found on the book of Acts. As I browsed through, I came across the book of Acts, Chapter 4 to be precise. In the next section, we will discuss the work of the apostles and how they came together to share whatever they could.

Acts 4:1-37 NIV: Peter and John Arrested

1 The priests and the captain of the temple guard and the
Sadducees came up to Peter and John while they were speaking
to the people. 2 They were greatly disturbed because the
apostles were teaching the people and proclaiming in Jesus the
resurrection of the dead. 3 They seized Peter and John and,
because it was evening, they put them in jail until the next day.
4 But many who heard the message believed, and the number of
men grew to about five thousand. 5 The next day the rulers,
elders and teachers of the law met in Jerusalem.

6 Annas the high priest was there, and so were Caiaphas, John,
Alexander and the other men of the high priest's family. 7 They
had Peter and John brought before them and began to question
them: "By what power or what name did you do this?" 8 Then
Peter, filled with the Holy Spirit, said to them: "Rulers and
elders of the people. 9 If we are being called to account today
for an act of kindness shown to a cripple and are asked how he
was healed,

10 then know this, you and all the people of Israel: It is by the
name of Jesus Christ of Nazareth, whom you crucified but
whom God raised from the dead, that this man stands before you
healed. 11 He is the stone you builders rejected, which has
become the capstone. 12 Salvation is found in no one else, for
there is no other name under heaven given to men by which we
must be saved."

13 When they saw the courage of Peter and John and realized
that they were unschooled, ordinary men, they were astonished
and they took note that these men had been with Jesus.

14 But since they could see the man who had been healed standing there with them, there was nothing they could say. 15 So they ordered them to withdraw from the Sanhedrin and then conferred together. 16" What are we going to do with these men?" they asked. "Everybody living in Jerusalem knows they have done an outstanding miracle, and we cannot deny it.

17 But to stop this thing from spreading any further among the people, we must warn these men to speak no longer to anyone in this name." 18 Then they called them in again and commanded them not to speak or teach at all in the name of Jesus. 19 But Peter and John replied, "Judge for yourselves whether it is right in God's sight to obey you rather than God. 20 For we cannot help speaking about what we have seen and heard.

21 After further threats they let them go. They could not decide how to punish them, because all the people were praising God for what had happened. 22 For the man who was miraculously healed was over forty years old. 23 On their release, Peter and John went back to their own people and reported all that the chief priests and elders had said to them. 24 When they heard this, they raised their voices together in prayer to God. "Sovereign Lord," they said, "you made the heaven and the earth and the sea, and everything in them.

25 You spoke by the Holy Spirit through the mouth of your servant, our father David: "why do the nations rage and the peoples plot in vain?" 26 The kings of the earth take their stand and the rulers gather together against the Lord and against his Anointed One. 27 Indeed Herod and Pontius Pilate met together with the Gentiles and the people of Israel in this city to conspire against your holy servant Jesus, whom you anointed.

28 They did what your power and will had decided beforehand should happen.

29 Now, Lord, consider their threats and enable your servants to speak your word with great boldness. 30 Stretch out your hand to heal and perform miraculous signs and wonders through the name of your holy servant Jesus." 31 After they prayed, the place where they were meeting was shaken.

And they were all filled with the Holy Spirit and spoke the word of God boldly. 32 All the believers were one in heart and mind. No one claimed that any of his possessions was his own, but they shared everything they had. 33 With great power the apostles continued to testify to the resurrection of the Lord Jesus, and much grace was upon them all.

34 There were no needy persons among them. For from time to time those who owned lands or houses sold them, brought the money from the sales 35 and put it at the apostles' feet, and it was distributed to anyone as he had need.

36 Joseph, a Levite from Cyprus, whom the apostles called Barnabas (which means Son of Encouragement), 37 sold a field he owned and brought the money and put it at the apostles' feet.

What happened when the apostles come together (assemble)?

   a) NIV Acts 4:2 "They were greatly disturbed because the apostles were teaching the people and proclaiming in Jesus the resurrection of the dead." Whenever the apostles assembled, they were teaching the word of God.

It is very important today that Christians learn from the apostles. We must assemble for a good purpose, not to destroy one another but to edify each other with the knowledge of God and Jesus Christ.

b) NIV Acts 4:31: "After they prayed, the place where they were meeting was shaken. And they were all filled with the Holy Spirit and spoke the word of God boldly". They spoke the word of God with boldness. It is important that, when we assemble as brethren, we pray for God's guidance, read the word and discuss the word so that we are familiar with the Bible.

That will help us to be bold when talking to other people, believers or non-believers. We should be able to answer any question with confidence. NLT Proverbs 6:21 says: "Keep the words always in your heart. Tie them around your neck."

c) NIV Acts 4:32: "All the believers were one in heart and mind. No one claimed that any of his possessions was his own, but they shared everything they had." When one reads this verse you feel pleased and sad at the same time. You feel pleased because sharing is caring and whenever the apostles and believers shared, no one lacked anything.

On the other hand, you feel sad because most brethren don't share nowadays. We have developed a spirit of greediness and have camouflaged it with the word "saving".

Hebrews 13:16 says, "And do not forget to do good and to share with others, for with such sacrifices God is pleased."

d) Acts 4: 33: "With great power the apostles continued to testify to the resurrection of the Lord Jesus, and much grace was upon them all." When we testify about Jesus, we don't only increase our faith but the faith of those listening to our testimony. 2 Timothy 1:8: "Therefore do not be ashamed of the testimony of our Lord or of me His prisoner, but join with me in suffering for the gospel according to the power of God."

Titus 3:3-7 English Standard Version (ESV) 3: For we ourselves were once foolish, disobedient, led astray, slaves to various passions and pleasures, passing our days in malice and envy, hated by others and hating one another.

4 But when the goodness and loving kindness of God our Saviour appeared, 5 he saved us, not because of works done by us in righteousness, but according to his own mercy, by the washing of regeneration and renewal of the Holy Spirit, 6 whom he poured out on us richly through Jesus Christ our Saviour, 7 so that being justified by his grace we might become heirs according to the hope of eternal life.

Testimonies are not only stories of God's wonderful works, but they are also the way we live now contrasted with our previous circumstances. Titus 3:3-7 beautifully sums up God's redemption and the ways He renews us as children of the Almighty God.

We testify to God's power, redeeming grace, and our new identity in Jesus Christ simply through our actions and choices we make.

It is a definitely a testimony of God's power when we shower love upon those who hurt and betray us, when we choose to think positively and trust God as our lives fall apart at the seams, and in the moments that we refuse temptations to fall back into our old habits or conform to the evils of this world.

Testimonies encourage others in their faith, and that is why it is crucial for Christians to share their testimony, even if they are new believers. You never know how sharing about your experiences can help others facing the same obstacles, or how the new person you've become can inspire others who seek to discover the God Who completely changed you.

These incredible stories don't have to be spoken in a crowded room over a speaker, but can simply arise during a conversation over a cup of coffee at Starbucks. Don't be afraid to divulge the messy details of your life to others — they may ultimately lead others to a relationship with God, one person at a time.

Source: https://www.theodysseyonline.com/sharing-our-testimony

Sharing your testimony with others is a must for all Christians. When giving your testimony, you tell how you came to trust in Christ alone as your Lord and Saviour. You tell how God opened your eyes to how you were a sinner in need of a Saviour.

When we testify, we are sharing with others different events leading up to our salvation and how God has worked in our lives to bring us to repentance. Testimony is a form of praise and honour to Christ.

We also use it as a way to encourage others. Know every time, when you're going through trials and sufferings in life, that it's an opportunity to share a testimony of how God worked in your life and made you stronger. Testimony is not only the things that we say. The way we live our life is a testimony to unbelievers as well.

Warning

We must be careful not to lie and exaggerate about things. We must be careful as well that we don't brag and glorify ourselves, which is what some people do, either on purpose or unknowingly. Instead of talking about Jesus, they use it as an opportunity to talk about themselves, which is no testimony at all. I'm pretty sure you heard people even bragging about their past life before Christ, as if it were cool.

I used to do this and that, I was a killer, I was making 10 000 dollars a month selling cocaine, blah blah blah -

and then Jesus. Examine your motives. It's all about Jesus and His glory. Don't make it about yourself.

Share today and build one another up because your testimony can have a huge impact on someone else's life.

Quotes and verses about testimony

1. Your story is the key that can unlock someone else's prison. "Only God can turn mess into a message, a test into a testimony, a trial into a triumph, a victim into a victory." What is my testimony? Jesus died. He was buried, and resurrected for our sins. 1 John 5:11: "This is the testimony: God has given us eternal life, and this life is found in his Son."

2. 1 John 5:10: "The one who believes in the Son of God has this testimony within him. The one who does not believe God has made Him a liar, because he has not believed in the testimony God has given about His Son." What does the Bible say about testimony?

3. Psalm 71:15-16: "I will declare your righteousness and your salvation every day, though I do not fully understand what the outcome will be. Lord God, I will come in the power of your mighty acts, remembering your righteousness—yours alone."

4. Mark 5:19: But Jesus said, "No, go home to your family, and tell them everything the Lord has done for you and how merciful he has been."

5. Psalm 22:22: "I will praise you to all my brothers; I will stand up before the congregation and testify of the wonderful things you have done."

6. Psalm 66:16: "Come and listen, all you who fear God, and I will tell you what he did for me."

7. John 15:26-27: "When the Helper comes, whom I will send to you from the Father— the Spirit of Truth, who comes from the Father—he will testify on my behalf. You will testify also, because you have been with me from the beginning. "

8. 1 John 1:2-3: "This life was revealed to us, and we have seen it and testify about it. We declare to you this eternal life that was with the Father and was revealed to us. What we have seen and heard we declare to you so that you, too, can have fellowship with us. Now this fellowship of ours is with the Father and with his Son, Jesus the Messiah."

9. Psalm 35:28: "My tongue will declare your righteousness and praise you all day long."

10. Daniel 4:2: "I want you all to know about the miraculous signs and wonders the Most High God has performed for me." Encourage each other by sharing testimonies."

11. 1 Thessalonians 5:11: "Wherefore comfort yourselves together, and edify one another, even as also ye do."

12. Hebrews 10:24-25: "And let us continue to consider how to motivate one another to love and good deeds, not neglecting to meet together, as is the habit of some, but encouraging one another even more as you see the day of the Lord coming nearer."

13. 1 Thessalonians 5:14: "We urge you, brothers, to admonish those who are idle, cheer up those who are discouraged, and help those who are weak. Be patient with everyone. Use your life as a testimony. Unbelievers will look closely at the life of a Christian."

14. Philippians 1:27-30: "Above all, you must live as citizens of heaven, conducting yourselves in a manner worthy of the Good News about Christ. Then, whether I come and see you again or only hear about you, I will know that you are standing together with one spirit and one purpose, fighting together for the faith, which is the Good News. Don't be intimidated in any way by your enemies.

This will be a sign to them that they are going to be destroyed, but that you are going to be saved, even by God himself. For you have been given not only the privilege of trusting in Christ but also the privilege of suffering for Him. We are in this struggle together. You have seen my struggle in the past, and you know that I am still in the midst of it."

15. Matthew 5:14-16: "You are light for the world. A city cannot be hidden when it is located on a hill. No one lights a lamp and puts it under a basket. Instead,

everyone who lights a lamp puts it on a lamp stand. Then its light shines on everyone in the house. In the same way let your light shine in front of people. Then they will see the good that you do and praise your Father in heaven."

16. 1 Peter 2:21: "To this you were called, because Christ suffered for you, leaving you an example that you should follow in his steps. Use your suffering as an opportunity to give a testimony." 17. Luke 21:12-13: But before all these things, people will arrest you and persecute you.

They will hand you over to synagogues and prisons, and you will be brought before kings and governors for my name's sake, in order to give you an opportunity to testify.

18. Philippians 1:12: "Now I want you to know, brothers and sisters, that what has happened to me has actually served to advance the gospel."

19. Philippians 1:12: "So I take pleasure in weaknesses, insults, catastrophes, persecutions, and in pressures, because of Christ. For when I am weak, then I am strong, unashamed of the gospel that saves."

20. 2 Timothy 1:8: "Therefore, never be ashamed of the testimony about our Lord or of me, his prisoner. Instead, by God's power, join me in suffering for the sake of the gospel."

21. Matthew 10:32: "Everyone who acknowledges me publicly here on earth, I will also acknowledge before my Father in heaven."

Reminders

22. Galatians 6:14: "But May I never boast about anything except the cross of our Lord Jesus, the Messiah, by which the world has been crucified to me, and I to the world."

23. 1 Corinthians 10:31: "Whether therefore ye eat, or drink, or whatsoever ye do, do all to the glory of God."

Examples

24. John 9:24-25: "So for the second time they called the man who had been blind and said to him, 'Give glory to God. We know that this man is a sinner.' He answered, 'Whether he is a sinner I do not know. One thing I do know, that though I was blind, now I see.'

25. Mark 5:20: "So the man started off to visit the Ten Towns of that region and began to proclaim the great things Jesus had done for him; and everyone was amazed at what he told them."

Source: https://biblereasons.com/testimony/

Bonus

Revelation 12:11: "They triumphed over him by the blood of the Lamb and by the word of their testimony; they did not love their lives so much as to shrink from death."

Assembling can either be the coming together for a good cause or for a bad cause. In the previous section we discussed the apostles assembling for a good cause, but in this section we will discuss coming together or assembling for the wrong reasons.

I'm reminded of a movie *The Italian Job*, which I was watching the other day on television. This is a perfect example of people meeting up for a wrong reason. We will discuss lessons learned from the plot of the movie at the end of this section. 1 Corinthians 15:33 says: "Do not be misled: 'Bad company corrupts good character.'"

The Italian Job (2003 Movie)

The Italian Job is a 2003 American heist film directed by F. Gary Gray and stars Mark Wahlberg, Charlize Theron, Edward Norton, Jason Statham, Seth Green, Mos Def and Donald Sutherland. It is the American remake of the 1969 British film of the same name, and is about a team of thieves who plan to steal gold from a former associate who double-crossed them.

The Plot

John Bridger, a professional safecracker, has assembled a team
to steal $35 million worth of gold bullion from a safe in Venice,
held by Italian gangsters who had stolen it weeks earlier. The
team includes Charlie Croker, a professional thief; Lyle or
"Napster", a computer expert; Handsome Rob, their wheelman;
Steve, their inside man; and Left Ear, their explosives expert.
The heist is successful but, as they drive towards Austria with
the bullion, they are stopped by men loyal to Steve, who had
turned on them and takes the bullion for himself.

Steve kills John when John admonishes him, and Rob drives the
van over a bridge into the waters below to protect the others,
using air tanks from the heist to stay alive. Steve leaves them for
dead. A year later in the United States, Charlie learns that Steve
has resurfaced under a new identity and is laundering the gold
through a Ukrainian jeweller named Yevhen to finance his
lavish lifestyle in Los Angeles.

Charlie gathers the team, and also recruits John's daughter
Stella, a skilled private safe cracker, offering her the chance to
get revenge on Steve for her father's death. They stake out
Steve's mansion and Stella, disguising herself as a cable
technician, is able to map out its interior, allowing them to
determine the location of Steve's safe containing the bullion.
Coincidentally, Steve, unaware of Stella's identity, offers to go
out on a date with her.

Charlie devises a plan using explosives to blow the safe while
Steve is away on his supposed date, using three heavily
modified Mini Coopers to transport the gold out of the mansion.

Charlie enlists the help of Skinny Pete for the explosives and
Wrench to make the modifications on the cars. However, on the
night of the planned heist, they find Steve's neighbours are
having a party and, as the explosives would draw their attention,
they abandon the plan.

Stella ends up having to meet Steve after all and inadvertently
gives away her identity to Steve by using phrases similar to the
ones her father used, but the team arrives to help protect her.
Steve is shocked that they had survived but taunts them that he
has the upper hand. Steve becomes paranoid that Charlie will
steal the gold, and starts to launder it faster, but he is forced to
kill Yevhen when he reveals his knowledge of the Venice heist.

Yevhen's death infuriates Mashkov, his cousin and a leading
member of a Ukrainian crime family. Mashkov connects the
murder to Charlie through Skinny Pete. Made more uneasy,
Steve makes plans to transport the gold to Mexico City by a
private plane from Los Angeles International Airport after
transporting it there in an armoured car.

Napster hears of this, and Charlie and his gang make a new plan
to steal the gold en route to the airport by hijacking the city's
traffic control system to force the armoured car to a planned spot
where they will execute the heist.

On the day of transport, they are surprised when three armoured
trucks leave Steve's mansion, but Napster is able to determine
which one is carrying the bullion, and manipulates the traffic
accordingly. Knowing that Steve is monitoring the transport by
helicopter, they get the car to the target spot and then create a
diversion as they detonate explosives to drop the part of the road

with the car into the old subway tunnels below. After opening the truck, they find a different safe to the one that held the gold before.

Although she struggles initially, Stella cracks the safe, and they load up the Coopers with the gold. They race from the subway to the Los Angeles River and through the city, pursued by Steve's henchmen on motorcycles, with Napster helping to create a green wave to evade traffic. Steve himself eventually leaves his helicopter and steals a truck to follow them to Union Station. At Union Station, the cars are loaded onto a train car with the help of Wrench.

Steve arrives shortly thereafter and, after bribing Wrench, is surprised to find Charlie and the others waiting for him. Steve brandishes a gun and demands his gold back, but Mashkov arrives. Charlie explains that he has offered Mashkov part of the gold and Steve in exchange for helping with security protection. Steve is punched in the face by Stella before being taken away by Mashkov, who reveals he will be tortured and killed.

The group boards the train as it departs to New Orleans, and celebrates in John's honour. The epilogue shows them all having used their share of the gold for their own desired purposes. Handsome Rob purchases an Aston Martin Vanquish, Left Ear buys a mansion in southern Spain, while Napster buys a powerful stereo capable of blowing a woman's clothes off.

Meanwhile, Charlie takes John's advice about finding someone he wants to spend the rest of his life with, and he and Stella travel to Venice. Source: https://en.m.wikipedia.org/wiki/The_Italian_Job_(2003_film)

Life lessons learned from the movie "*The Italian Job*" about bad company (assembling for the wrong reasons):

a) Here we learn that bad company always has wrong motives. Psalm 1:1: "Blessed is the one who does not walk in step with the wicked or stand in the way that sinners take or sit in the company of mockers". The movie is about a team of thieves who plan to steal gold from a former associate who double-crossed them. Already you can tell that there was betrayal involved and that stealing is thus inevitable as a tool for revenge on the associate who double-crossed the thieves.

b) Here we see John Bridger, a professional safecracker, who assembled a team to steal $35 million worth of gold bullion from a safe in Venice, held by Italian gangsters who had stolen it weeks earlier. It is said that teamwork is the ability to work together toward a common vision and we see it in the movie, which brings us to the conclusion that a common vision is not always a good vision. Romans 12:2: "Do not be conformed to this world, but be transformed by the renewing of your mind, so that you may prove what the will of God is, that which is good and acceptable and perfect."

c) We also see Charlie gathering the team, and recruiting John's daughter Stella, a skilled private safe cracker, offering her the chance to get revenge on Steve for her father's death. Revenge is on the cards here, as we can see Charlie's actions are about "an eye for an eye". He is using Stella as an excuse for his actions. The Bible, however, teaches us about forgiveness, loving your neighbour as yourself, and that is the biggest reason Jesus died for our sins: so that we are forgiven. 1 Peter 3:9: "Do not repay evil with evil or insult with insult. On the contrary, repay evil with blessing, because to this you were called so that you may inherit a blessing."

d) Steve becomes paranoid that Charlie will steal the gold, and starts to launder it faster, but he is forced to kill Yevhen when he reveals his knowledge of the Venice heist. Here we see a power struggle: Steve and Charlie are power hungry. Steve is suspicious of Charlie stealing the gold and, because there is mistrust among them, it leads to the killing of Yevhen because he knew something about Steve's dirty past. We can learn from this that, because the team gathers for bad motives, mistrust is inevitable among them: no one trusts anyone. Psalm 188:8: "It is better to take refuge in the LORD than to trust in man."

e) We see Steve arriving shortly thereafter and, after bribing Wrench, he is surprised to find Charlie and the others waiting for him. There is a popular quote by **Suzy Kassem** which says; *"In these times, a great leader must be extremely brave. His leadership must be steered only by his conscience, not a bribe."* Steve was a leader of the team but here he is showing desperation by bribing. He is bribing Wrench because the team is now stealing from him.

f) We learn that a bad vision in life leads to bad choices and bad choices leads ultimately to a bad ending or even death, so we must choose wisely.

2 Chronicles 19:7: "Now then let the fear of the LORD be upon you; be very careful what you do, for the LORD our God will have no part in unrighteousness or partiality or the taking of a bribe."

g) They celebrated, even though a lot of people lost their lives along the way. It's a lesson that people love gold or money so much that they have lost compassion, respect and kindness. They are prepared to be rich, even if death is what it takes. Proverbs 11:4: "Wealth is worthless in the day of wrath, but righteousness delivers from death."

INSPIRING: CHAPTER 3

Thirdly, to be positively influential in your Christian life and faith, you must be *inspiring* towards other brethren in order for you and them to grow spiritually. I would like to start by defining the word inspirational. According to the Cambridge Dictionary; inspiring means:

a) "Encouraging, or making you feel you want to do something."

b) "Causing you feel confident about yourself or eager to learn or do something."

https://www.biblestudytools.com/topical-verses/faith-bible-verses/ : It is so easy to face new failures and fears and to lose faith in God's plan for your life. We begin to question if God is real and if He cares about us. "I want to encourage you with the truth that I the Creator and Sustainer am working in and through you while you go through struggles"

I have come across great men and women of faith in my life, but one specifically comes to mind. Fr. Martin McCormack is a very positive man who always aspires to inspire. He has his favourite line (paraphrasing): "Impossible doesn't exist in my vocabulary. To me, impossible means: "I'm-possible." In short, don't let any negativity engulf your thoughts lest you fail.

Always think about yourself as a winner, as a successful person, and as someone who has already achieved whatever your heart desires. Never let success blind you, but always be content with whatever you have and don't forget to be generous because it is not guaranteed that what you have today you will still have tomorrow".

As we discuss inspiring, I'm reminded of a sermon I shared at Zombodze Apostolic Faith Church on the 28th of October 2018. The title of the sermon was "Perseverance". It was a faith motivational sermon which encouraged brethren not to give up on their faith.

I am tempted to share the sermon because every time I read it on my laptop I feel so motivated and have huge courage that whatever situation or obstacles I may face, God is at work. God will never leave us or forsake us and no burden will be too heavy for us to carry. Luke 1:37: "For nothing will be impossible with God". Please see the sermon below and I hope you will be inspired as you read through.

Sermon Title: ***Perseverance***

Date: 28/10/2018

By: Mr. B Mkhonta

Venue: Zombodze Apostolic Faith Church (Kingdom of ESwatini)

Romans 5:3 - 4: "And not only that, but we also glory in tribulations, knowing that tribulation produces perseverance; and perseverance, character; and character, hope."

Romans 8:25: "But if we hope for what we do not see, we eagerly wait for it with perseverance."

2 Timothy 3:10 – "But you have carefully followed my doctrine, manner of life, purpose, faith, longsuffering, love, perseverance."

Three facts about suffering:

   a) You are suffering at the moment.

   b) You have suffered before.

   c) You will suffer in the near future.

Six Faith-sustaining purposes of God in our suffering:

   1. **Repentance**: Suffering is a call for us and others to turn from treasuring anything on earth above God. Luke 13:4–5: "Or those eighteen on whom the tower in Siloam fell and killed them: do you think that they were worse offenders than all the others who lived in Jerusalem? No, I tell you; but unless you repent, you will all likewise perish."

   2. **Reliance**: Suffering is a call to trust God and not the life-sustaining props of this world. 2 Corinthians 1:8–9: "We were so utterly burdened beyond our strength that we despaired of life itself. Indeed, we felt that we had received the sentence of death. But that was to make us rely not on ourselves but on God who raises the dead."

   3. **Righteousness**: Suffering is the discipline of our loving heavenly Father so that we come to share His righteousness and holiness. Hebrews 12:6, 10–11:

"The Lord disciplines the one he loves, and chastises every son whom he receives." He disciplines us for our own good, that we may share His holiness.

For the moment, all discipline seems painful rather than pleasant, but later it yields the peaceful fruit of righteousness to those who have been trained by it.

4. **To make God proud**: Suffering makes God proud of us once we conquer the devil. Job 1: 6 -12, Job 1:8: "Then the Lord said to Satan, 'Have you considered My servant Job, that there is none like him on the earth, a blameless and upright man, and one who fears God and shuns evil?'"

5. **Reward:** Suffering is working for us a great reward in heaven that will make up for every loss here a thousand fold. James 1:12: "Blessed is the man who endures temptation; for when he has been approved, he will receive the crown of life which the Lord has promised to those who love Him."

6. Finally, **Resist the devil**: Suffering makes us stronger and more experienced about life. We become stronger in resisting the devil. 1 Peter 5:8-10: "Resist him, steadfast in the faith, knowing that the same sufferings are experienced by your brotherhood in the world."

So, it is understandable that the Christian heart will cry out in suffering, "Why?" since we don't know most of the micro reasons for our suffering — why now, why this way, why this long? But don't let that ignorance of the micro reasons cause you to overlook the massive help God gives in His word by telling us his macro purposes for us.

Source: https://www.desiringgod.org/articles/five-purposes-for-suffering

What I have learned from the sermon "*Perseverance*"

a) Romans 8:18: "For I consider that the sufferings of this present time are not worthy to be compared with the glory which shall be revealed in us. "

   I figured out that the reasons we face trials and tribulations are:

   - to make us stronger and much more pure and righteous;
   - to shape our way of reasoning;
   - to give us experience;
   - to help us survive throughout our lives;
   - because God allows temptations and trials for a purpose;
   - to teach us to be patient.

b) The three facts about suffering are impossible to escape as long as you are alive;

   - ***You are suffering at the moment***: 1 Peter 1:7 ESV: "…so that the tested genuineness of you faith - more precious than gold that perishes though it is tested by fire - may be found to result in praise and glory and honour at the revelation of Jesus Christ."

- ***You have suffered before***: 1 Peter 4:12 NKJV: "Beloved, do not think it strange concerning the fiery trial which is to try you, as though some strange thing happened to you."

- ***You will suffer in the near future***: John 16:33 NKJV: "These things I have spoken to you, that in Me you may have peace. In the world you will have tribulation; but be of good cheer, I have overcome the world."

c) ***My testimony***: I shared a short testimony when I was preaching and I thought maybe I could put it on record by writing it down in this section about trials and tribulations. I shared the testimony about my daughter Thubalenkosi Abigail Mkhonta. I remember the day she was born. I woke up on the morning of the 28th of April 2018 and everything looked normal.

I went to the shop to get something to prepare our breakfast. On that day, my sister-in-law and my mother-in-law were with us in the house.

I don't usually leave my cellphone when I go out, and especially not at that time because my wife was heavily pregnant. That morning, for whatever reason, I left it on the charger. My wife called me and it rang next to her in the bedroom. When I came back, about thirty minutes later, I found her dressing and our bed was full of blood.

One thing that came to my mind was that we were going to lose the baby. I was panicking, but my wife was calm. She didn't even inform my in-laws, who were in the house at that time.

I knew that the she was due to give birth in a week's time or so but not so soon. The baby's clothes were packed already and we drove to Mediclinic in Trichardt. When we arrived, it was a matter of emergency and I tried to be calm outside but inside I was nervous.

God showed His love in that all went well and the baby was born healthy an hour later at 11:30 am. We were facing our own trials but God wanted us to trust Him even more and we were so grateful to God. Isaiah 41:13 "For I am the LORD your God who takes hold of your right hand and says to you, Do not fear; I will help you."

My life experiences: *Growing up and school life*

I was born on the 10th of December 1985. A lot has happened in my life. I've had some good experiences and some bad ones too, but throughout everything I've never lost my faith in God and Jesus Christ and all the promises He makes to us throughout the scriptures in the Bible. I will share some experiences of mine and I hope they will inspire someone somewhere who is going through the same thing.

We learn from past experiences. Present experiences help us to appreciate life, and future experiences will help us to endure whatever life throws at us. Jeremiah 29:11 NIV: "For I know the plans I have for you," declares the LORD, "plans to prosper you and not to harm you, plans to give you hope and future."

Growing up for me was not easy. In fact, my parents were not around.

I was told by my late grandfather from my mother's side (Malayisha Sifundza), that my father never took care of me. When I was born, he left for South Africa to work in the mines and he had a lot of girlfriends at that time so he was never in my life at all. My mother got married and she was happy with her husband and their kids.

I wondered why I was not attending any school and my grandfather told me that he was unable to pay for my school fees. As a child it's difficult to understand such things.

I only attended a school designed for illiterate people (kaSebenta), who'd never got a chance to go to be in the normal schooling curriculum system, when I was about eight years old.

It was not even a proper school. We learned under a tree and when it was raining we were not able to attend school. There was no proper syllabus we were following per se. We just learned practical things about life, for example agriculture, woodwork and sewing. I could feel that this was not for me but I had no choice but to attend the school because my grandfather could afford to pay for me.

I used to look after the cattle as well, so attending the school was not an everyday task. I was behind at school all the time but during the time I got a chance to attend I used to catch up and be top of the class in my marks. I was the youngest in the class (under the gum tree) and I was treated very well by my classmates, even thought they were older than me - some of them were my parents' age.

Fast forward to 1994. My grandfather couldn't afford to pay and take care of me, so he sent me to stay with his brother and look after his brother's cattle too. My grandfather thought that by going to stay with his brother I would assist them with the looking after of the cattle and in return I would be assisted in paying for my school fees and for my school uniform - but that never happened.

I looked after the cattle without pay for the whole year and I was unable to attend school the following year so my grandmother Esther Dlamini, from my father's side, took me to stay with her and she promised that I would not be looking after cattle or any livestock and I would be able to attend school.

I was able to start school at Ludzeludze Primary School in 1996, I was in Grade 1 for a week before I was promoted to Standard 1 (Grade 3) and I was 10 years turning 11 that same year. I got position 19 during the second term in Standard 1 and position 4 at the end of the year overall. From Standard 2 to Standard 5 (Grade 7) I was always in position 1 in class.

The years passed so fast but they didn't go without any challenges as I was sent home several times because I couldn't afford school fees. But, through the grace of God I was able to sell paw paws and vegetables in order for me to go to school. I was working on our neighbours' maize fields, helping them weed or harvest, and they paid me for my efforts.

My grandmother always made sure that my older sister Bongekile and I had food. There were some times when we used to go to bed without food, and life wasn't easy, but what drove me was my positive attitude in a nearly impossible situation. I knew God was there and I knew He gave me a bright mind to excel at school and I was going to be successful, no matter what.

There was a time when I thought I would never finish my primary school but throughout all the trials and tribulations I was able to obtain a "first class" on my Standard 5 (Grade 7) external final examination results. The struggle continued again when I attended my high school at Salesian High School in Manzini.

I applied at Salesian and I was accepted because of my good results. I never thought I would ever do my high school at Salesian; it was every boy's dream to go to Salesian High School because of the good reputation the school had for results at that time. It was a boy's school so it excelled in sports. I didn't have money to pay for the deposit in Form 1 so that I would be able to attend classes and receive my books and uniform. The school offered uniforms to the students only after the deposit have been paid.

I had to find some means. After I'd tried everything and nothing materialized, I decided to go to the national television station (Swazi TV/eSwatini TV) and the national newspaper (the *Times of Swaziland*) requesting and seeking for some help. I did interviews with both media channels and God answered my prayers. Someone in South Africa decided to pay for my deposit anonymously, through the *Times of Swaziland* after reading my story in that paper. It was a week before schools commenced for

that year (2001) so when I received the call for the times of
Swaziland I knew that God was still with me.

My high school days were never easy. It was getting tougher
and tougher to obtain any academic funding and by that time,
unlike in primary where I used to walk to school, I had to get
into a bus every morning to go to school because Salesian High
School is in Manzini town, so it was far from home. In terms of
performance in class, I dropped from being a top student to and
average performance because of the challenges I had financially.
I was struggling to even get money for transport so I had to
continue working on our neighbours' fields to help them with
whatever they requested me to do in order to get money for
transport.

It was not always the case that I would be able to get money
every weekend so Mrs. Glory Vilakati used to intervene by
giving me bus fare and food sometimes when I had nothing to
eat. I remember I was not able to pay my school fees balance in
Form 1 and Mr. Rocky Mabaso, the then deputy school principal
at Salesian, helped me not to pay and to proceed to Form 2
because I had done well in Form 1, regardless of the challenges.
My grandmother went to Durban, South Africa, with my sister
to stay with my aunt, Dum'sile, for two years and I was alone
without food, school uniform or money for transport and money
for my school fees.

My grandmother moved me out of her house before she left for
Durban because she wanted to lock the house and make sure it
was secured. I moved out to a shack with all my clothes, pots
and my school books. When it rained my books got wet and my
bed would be swamped with water dripping through the shack's

roof. Mr. Douglas Vilakati would then come and ask me to sleep at his house because my shack was flooded. Throughout all the challenges, I was able to pass my Form 2 and I finished the year without paying my school fees and my bus fares were paid by Mrs. Glory Vilakati, as I mentioned earlier.

The following year, the same school fee challenge continued. I went to Salesian to meet up with Mr. Rocky Mabaso and he told me not to worry about the Form 2 school fees. The school was going to pay for me through the orphanage fund. He said that I should return to school to do my Form 3. The only struggle I had was the bus fare and food, and I used to miss class due to lack of funds. When it happened that I was able to attend school, I had the challenge of not having been able to eat and I was being hugely affected academically. Against all odds, in 2003 I was able to obtain a second class on my external final examination in Form 3.

The situation was not getting any better so I decided to drop out of school and in 2004 I never return to school. I tried to look for a job so that I would be able to continue with my Form 4 studies in 2005. My aunt in Durban decided to offer me a job at her restaurant. I worked there for the whole of 2004 in the hope that I could return to school the following year to do my Form 4 and proceed to Form 5 the year after. Working in a restaurant was not something I'd thought I'd land up doing, but I did. The year seemed to be moving in a snail's pace because I was hungry to go back to school the following year.

It was not easy to see other children attending school while I was working in the restaurant, but I knew that it was not my dream job. I dreamt of becoming a scientist, mathematician or else an engineer in the physics field and that drive kept me going. I refused to see myself as someone who was illiterate and working in a restaurant, so my faith in God grew. I trusted Him even more, praying all the time for my situation to change for the better.

The excitement increased towards the end of 2004 because I knew I was going back to school and I felt in my spirit that I was going to make it in life. I was going to be what I wanted to be. God gave me an academic brain, so I was going to use well. I was constantly reminded of the story of talents in the Bible and that one day we have to account for our unused talents before God (Matthew 25:14-30).

In 2005, Mr. Rocky Mabaso and the late Mr. Jeremiah Ginindza (may his soul rest in peace), introduced me to Fr. Martin McCormack and that was the beginning of great things to come. Fr. Martin sponsored me and paid for my Form 4 and 5 years respectively. He also paid for my transport fees and food for the remaining two years of my high school. He was indeed heavenly sent to me. I was performing well in class and Mr. Jeremiah Ginindza made me join the "A" class from the "D" class. The "A" class was the most hardworking and had super brilliant students at that time. That motivated me to do even better academically, because the competition was very high.

The class of 2006 at Salesian High School did extremely well and I was very pleased to be among the students who credited every subject. I obtained a "B" aggregate overall and a 19 score line on the Cambridge O-level score board. I was so excited when I received my letter of acceptance from the post office that stated that I had been accepted at the University of Swaziland/

ESwatini (UNISWA/UNESWA). Until then, it had been only a dream to me. I'd never thought it was really possible for someone of my background to even finish Form 5, let alone enrol at the highest tertiary education campus in Swaziland.

After being awarded a scholarship by the Swazi government, I enrolled on the JMC course, which was a Journalism and Mass Communication course. I was enjoying the course and excelling in my class, but being a top student in a course I wasn't sure was the right one for me made me to come to the conclusion that I had to pursue a career in Technology, because I was more technically minded than scholastically minded.

I left the University of Swaziland in 2006 after just one semester and pursued Information Technology, the career of my dreams, at CTI Durban campus in South Africa in 2007. With the assistance of Fr. Martin McCormack, who continued to support me with funding, I was able to enrol at CTI after excelling in the aptitude test required before enrolling.

I graduated two years later, receiving an award for the top achiever overall in the courses. I was awarded an International Diploma in Computer Studies and BTEC HND in Information Technology Level 5i, obtaining distinctions and merits respectively.

I am reminded of a verse in the Bible - 2 Corinthians 12:9-11 NIV: "But He said to me, My grace is sufficient for you, for my power is made perfect in weakness. Therefore, I will boast all the more gladly about my weakness, so that Christ's power may rest on me. That is why, for Christ's sake, I delight in weakness, in insults, in hardship, in persecutions, in difficulties. For when I am weak, then I am strong."

Philippians 4:6: "Do not be anxious about anything, but in every situation, by prayer and petition, with thanksgiving, present your requests to God." This was my theme verse throughout my school life. I wouldn't have achieved anything without God and He is faithful. When I look back to reflect on the many challenges I faced and conquered in the past, I am reminded of Bishop Tshalo Katshunga's sermon in Cape Town.

He said (paraphrasing): "Whatever life throws at you, either bad or good, just make sure that you hold on. There has never been a permanent situation in life. The only thing you need to do is just to hang in there because God hasn't forgotten about you."

There have been so many people who contributed to my academic success throughout the years. Whether small or huge contributions, to me they contributed equally because without any of their contributions I wouldn't have made it at all, let alone graduated. I'm grateful to you, my grandmother Esther Dlamini, for giving me shelter, feeding me and contributing the little you had towards my primary school education. You are an unsung heroine; even though you didn't get the chance to go far at school you wanted your children and grandchildren to be educated. Your contributions changed me from being a boy to a man; you taught me how to survive in life at a tender age and for that I will forever be indebted to you.

To my aunts, Fortunate Mkhonta and Dum'sile Malambe: you played a huge role in that, when I was studying in Durban, I used to stay with Aunt Dumi, who contributed towards my transport, food and shelter. My Aunt Fortunate contributed vegetables, money and maize meal when we were starving. I used to sell some of the vegetables to contribute towards my school fees in primary school.

Neither of my aunts had much. They have children of their own to take care of but, unselfishly, they contributed towards my academic life and for that I will forever be grateful and can't thank them enough. I know God will see to their needs and bless them profusely. Proverbs 19:17: "Whoever is generous to the poor lends to the Lord, and He will repay him for his deed."

My uncle, the late Sabelo Moses Dube, taught me that nothing comes for free. You have to work hard in order to be successful. He used to pay for my fees in primary school and he was really a father figure in my life. He motivated me in many ways; he was a product of Salesian High School himself, so he convinced me to apply at Salesian because it was the best performing school academically at that time in Swaziland.

I used to work in his fields. He farmed vegetables commercially so I took care of the vegetables on weekends and during school holidays and for that I will always cherish his contributions. Proverbs 12:11 "Those who work their land will have abundant food, but those who chase fantasies have no sense."

To all the heroes and heroines who contributed towards my academic life, I will always be grateful I hope that by sharing this summary of my academic life, someone's spirit will be uplifted, that someone who is about to give up in life will persevere. There is no permanent situation in life, no matter how painful and difficult it maybe.

"Being defeated is often a temporary condition. Giving up is what makes it permanent." – **Marilyn vos Savant**

Be inspired by the story of Job in the Bible

Just about everyone has heard of the suffering of Job in the Old Testament. You might have heard someone say, "They have the patience of Job." There is good reason for that saying. According to biblical scholars, the Book of Job is the oldest book in the Bible. If you were to fit it chronologically, it should be placed in the early chapters of Genesis. What can we learn from the Book of Job? Is there application for the believer's life today? Was sin involved in Job's suffering? Is there sin in all suffering? Why does God allow suffering?

The Accuser

All was going well with Job. He had it all: a large family, wealth and blessings of every kind imaginable. At that time, Job may have been the richest man on the face of the earth. Job 1:2-3 describes his wealth as: "He had seven sons and three daughters, and he owned seven thousand sheep, three thousand camels, five hundred yoke of oxen and five hundred donkeys, and had a large number of servants. He was the greatest man among all the people of the East." Clearly, Job had it all.

This must have bothered Satan because he came to God. What did God say to Satan about Job? God bragged about Job in 1:8: "Then the LORD said to Satan, "Have you considered my servant Job? There is no one on earth like him; he is blameless and upright, a man who fears God and shuns evil."

Can you imagine the God of the Universe bragging about Job from heaven? Might He also brag about you and your righteousness, found in Jesus Christ? It is entirely possible. However, Satan was not convinced and said to God,

"Does Job fear God for nothing? Have you not put a hedge around him and his household and everything he has? You have blessed the work of his hands, so that his flocks and herds are spread throughout the land. But now stretch out your hand and strike everything he has, and he will surely curse you to your face" (Job 1:9-11).

Satan's name means "adversary" and he has been called the "accuser of the brethren" (Rev. 12:10). So, God sets out to prove to Satan that Job is not righteous just because he is being blessed.

God challenges the Devil telling him, "Very well, then, everything he has is in your power, but on the man himself do not lay a finger" (Job 1:12). Job lost just about everything: his sheep, his oxen, his camels, his servants, and all of his sons and daughters – but remarkably he did not lose his faith in God. What was Job's response?

"Then Job arose, tore his robe, and shaved his head; and he fell to the ground and worshiped. And he said: "Naked I came from my mother's womb, and naked shall I return there. The LORD gave, and the LORD has taken away; Blessed be the name of the LORD. In all this, Job did not sin nor charge God with wrong" (Job 1:20-22). Here we can plainly see Job's reaction. He worshiped God, he said that he came into this world with nothing and would return with nothing. The Lord has taken away all he had except his wife – and his wife told him to "curse God and die" – but Job blessed the name of the Lord. In all of this, "Job did not sin nor charge God with wrong."

He blessed God's name, he worshiped God, and he did not sin. Satan must have been angry at Job's response. Job suffered unjustly and yet he did not blame God or say, "Why me?"

Job's Fair-weather Friends

Job's friends tried to console him but they soon started to blame him for his own troubles, inferring that he must have sinned in order for all these trials to come upon him. That is something that is far too easy for believers to do. When they see a Christian suffer, they unfairly assume that there must be sin in that believer's life.

But suffering is not always a result of sin, as we see with Job. In many cases, those who are sinners suffer little while those who are saints suffer much. Many people see this as a stumbling block for Christianity and ask why God allows suffering. Instead of asking "why" they might be better off asking "what". What is God up to? What is He trying to produce in us? Like the refiner's fire, God often uses suffering to produce righteous character in believers. Sometimes, He wants those who suffer to be more dependent upon Him.

It may be that He is trying to get our attention. We might even be sinning; however, we cannot always equate suffering with sin in a believer's life as we see with Job's experience. At first, Job's friends try to help Job but they quickly turn to accusing him of some sort of hidden or known sin. Job knows that this is

not the reason and tries to justify himself against their
accusations. But his justification quickly turns to self-
righteousness and that is a sin before God.

Job's friends say, "Is not your wickedness great? Are not your
sins endless? You demanded security from your brothers for no
reason; you stripped men of their clothing, leaving them naked.
You gave no water to the weary and you withheld food from the
hungry, though you were a powerful man, owning land– an
honoured man, living on it. And you sent widows away empty-
handed and broke the strength of the fatherless. That is why
snares are all around you, why sudden peril terrifies you" (Job
22:5-10). This brings God's righteous indignation upon Job's
friends (Job 42:7-17).

God Answers Job

Job is not guiltless, as no man is without sin (1 John 1:8,
Romans 3:23). Job becomes discouraged, partly because of the
blame game played by his friends. Job begins to question God
and this is when God answers Job out of the whirlwind
(tornado?). He says, "Who is this who darkens counsel by words
without knowledge? Now prepare yourself like a man; I will
question you, and you shall answer Me. Where were you when I
laid the foundations of the earth? Tell Me, if you have
understanding" (Job 38:2-4).

God puts Job in his place and in effect tells Job, "Who are you
to question the God of the Universe?" God never does answer
Job's question about why He allows suffering. God, in His
sovereignty, chooses not to tell us everything. That is God's
prerogative. Also notice that God spoke to Job out of the

"whirlwind", which is the terminology for a tornado or great and destructive windstorm. This could indicate that God is in all things going on this world. He is sovereign and nothing happens that is not within His perfect will. These things include natural disasters and calamities. God is never caught off guard or by surprise.

Someday in eternity, God will likely make it clear why Christians suffer – why something terrible was allowed to happen or why their child was allowed to die. It is as God once said in Isaiah 45:9; "Woe to him who quarrels with his Maker, to him who is but a potsherd among the potsherds on the ground. Does the clay say to the potter, 'What are you making?' Does your work say, 'He has no hands'?

We cannot question God's motives. His ways are beyond human comprehension but clearly He does have a purpose in suffering. As God tells Isaiah, "As the heavens are higher than the earth, so are my ways higher than your ways and my thoughts than your thoughts" (Isaiah. 55:9). He sometimes chooses not to reveal this to believers – at least in this life.

God Restores Job

If Job had known that God would have restored to him more than he had in the first place, would he have questioned Him at all? God rewards Job for his faithfulness and his endurance through such suffering. This story has an incredible ending.

Job 42:10-17: "After Job had prayed for his friends, the LORD restored his prosperity and doubled his [previous] possessions. All his brothers, sisters and former acquaintances came to his house and dined with him in his house. They offered him sympathy and comfort concerning all the adversity the LORD had brought on him. Each one gave him a qesitah and a gold earring.

So the LORD blessed the latter part of Job's life more than the earlier. He owned 14 000 sheep, 6 000 camels, 1 000 yoke of oxen and 1 000 female donkeys. He also had seven sons and three daughters.

He named his first [daughter] Jemimah, his second Keziah, and his third Keren-happuch. No women as beautiful as Job's daughters could be found in all the land and their father granted them an inheritance with their brothers. Job lived 140 years after this and saw his children and their children to the fourth generation. "Then Job died, old and full of days."

So Job ended up much better off than he was in the beginning. He had considerably more than when he began his suffering and, even though God did not answer Job about why he was allowed to suffer so terribly, in the end Job had more blessings than any man on the face of the earth at that time.

The application for Christians today is that God will bless those who endure to the end and that someday God will reward us with unbelievable blessings that cannot compare with what we have today (Rom 8:18, 28). We will all suffer in this life. It is appointed to mankind to suffer. It is a fallen world. We may not know the "why" today, but some day we probably will. Instead of asking "why", we should ask "what". What is God up to?

What is God trying to do in me? The "why" will have to wait
for some day in eternity. Until then, we cannot fully grasp the
purpose of God but we know that He will not allow us to suffer
into eternity. One thing that is important is that Satan could not
lay a finger on Job, nor can he harm us. God will not allow this
(Job 1:12. I John 4:4).

Those who reject God today, may have suffering in this life and
in the after-life. For those who believe in Him today and trust in
the Son of God, their suffering will be over someday. They will
have eternal joy and fellowship with God. My prayer for you is
that you can inherit this eternal joy where there will be no more
sorrow, no more pain, no more suffering and no more death.

Let the Word of God tell us what is in store for the children of
God some day in Revelation 21:4: "He will wipe every tear
from their eyes. There will be no more death or mourning or
crying or pain, for the old order of things has passed away." By
Jack Wellman:
https://www.whatchristianswanttoknow.com/job-bible-story-
summary-with-lesson/.

What can we learn from the life of Job?

1. The life of Job demonstrates that humans are often unaware
of the many ways God is at work in the life of each believer.
Job's life is also one that prompts the common question, **"Why
do bad things happen to good people?"**

It is the age-old question, and difficult to answer, but believers
know that God is always in control, and, no matter what
happens, there are no coincidences—nothing happens by

chance. Job was a believer; he knew that God was on the throne and in total control, though he had no way of knowing why so many terrible tragedies were occurring in his life.

2. Job was "blameless and upright; he feared God and shunned evil" (Job 1:1). He had ten children and was a man of great wealth. The Bible tells us that one day Satan presented himself before God and God asked Satan what he thought of Job. Satan accused Job of honouring God only because God had blessed him. So, God allowed Satan to take away Job's wealth and his children. Later, God allowed Satan to afflict Job physically. Job grieved deeply but did not charge God with wrongdoing (Job 1:22; 42:7–8).

3. Job's friends were certain that Job must have sinned in order to deserve punishment and argued with him about it. But Job maintained his innocence, though he confessed that he wanted to die and did ask questions of God.

A younger man, Elihu, attempted to speak on God's behalf before God, Himself, answered Job. Job 38—42 contain some of the most stunning poetry about the magnitude and might of God. Job responded to God's discourse in humility and repentance, saying he had spoken of things he did not know (Job 40:3–5; 42:1–6).

God told Job's friends that He was angry with them for speaking falsehoods about Him, unlike Job who had spoken truth (Job 42:7–8). God told them to offer sacrifices and that Job would pray on their behalf and God would accept Job's prayer. Job did so, likely forgiving his friends for their harshness himself. God restored Job's fortunes two-fold (Job 42:10) and "blessed the latter part of Job's life more than the former part" (Job 42:12). Job lived 140 years after his suffering.

4. Job never lost his faith in God, even under the most heart-breaking circumstances that tested him to his core. It's hard to imagine losing everything we own in one day—property, possessions, and even children. Most men would sink into depression and perhaps even become suicidal after such massive loss. Though depressed enough to curse the day of his birth (Job 3:1–26), Job never cursed God (Job 2:9–10) nor did he waver in his understanding that God was still in control.

Job's three friends, on the other hand, instead of comforting him, gave him bad advice and even accused him of committing sins so grievous that God was punishing him with misery.

Job knew God well enough to know that He did not work that way; in fact, he had such an intimate, personal relationship with Him that he was able to say, "Though he slay me, yet will I hope in him; I will surely defend my ways to his face" (Job 13:15). When Job's wife suggested he curse God and die, Job replied "You are talking like a foolish woman. Shall we accept good from God, and not trouble?" (Job 2:10).

5. Job's plight, from the death of his children and loss of his property to the physical torment he endured, plus the harangue of his so-called friends, never caused his faith to waver. He knew who his Redeemer was. He knew that He was a living Saviour, and he knew that someday He would physically stand on the earth (Job 19:25). He understood that man's days are ordained (numbered) and they cannot be changed (Job 14:5). The spiritual depth of Job shows throughout the book.

James refers to Job as an example of perseverance, writing, "Brothers and sisters, as an example of patience in the face of suffering, take the prophets who spoke in the name of the Lord. As you know, we count as blessed those who have persevered. You have heard of Job's perseverance and have seen what the Lord finally brought about. The Lord is full of compassion and mercy" (James 5:10–11).

6. There are also several scientific and historical facts in the book of Job. The book implied the earth is round long before the advent of modern science (Job 22:14). The book mentions dinosaurs—not by that name, but the description of the behemoth is certainly dinosaur-like—living side by side with man (Job 40:15–24).

7. The book of Job gives us a glimpse behind the veil that separates earthly life from the heavenly. In the beginning of the book, we see that Satan and his fallen angels are still allowed access to heaven, going in and out to the prescribed meetings that take place there. What is obvious from these accounts is that Satan is busy working his evil on earth, as recorded in Job 1:6-7.

Also, this account shows how Satan is "the accuser of the brethren," which corresponds to Revelation 12:10, and it shows his arrogance and pride, as written in Isaiah 14:13–14. It is amazing to see how Satan challenges God; he has no scruples about confronting the Most High. The account in Job shows Satan as he truly is—haughty and evil to the core.

8. Perhaps the greatest lesson we learn from the book of Job is that God does not have to answer to anyone for what He does or does not do. Job's experience teaches us that we may never

know the specific reason for suffering, but we must trust in our sovereign, holy, righteous God. His ways are perfect (Psalm 18:30). Since God's ways are perfect, we can trust that whatever He does—and whatever He allows—is also perfect.

We can't expect to understand God's mind perfectly. As He reminds us, "For my thoughts are not your thoughts, neither are your ways my ways… For as the heavens are higher than the earth, so are my ways higher than your ways and my thoughts than your thoughts" (Isaiah 55:8–9).

9. Our responsibility to God is to obey Him, to trust Him, and to submit to His will, whether we understand it or not. When we do, we will find God in the midst of our trials—possibly even because of our trials. We will see more clearly the magnificence of our God, and we will say, with Job, "My ears had heard of you but now my eyes have seen you" (Job 42:5).

Source: https://www.gotquestions.org/life-Job.html

In Conclusion

1. *Bad things happen to good people*

Despite living a righteous and obedient life, Job was met with many trials, including the loss of property and of all his children. Even Job's friends started accusing him of being a wicked man; they insisted that his trials and hardships were a punishment from God.

Job didn't let the setbacks of life discourage him or weaken his faith. We won't always know the reasons why hardships enter our life or why bad things happen to us. Having the knowledge that trials can be a source of strength and experience helps us face our trials. Through these experiences, we are able to better understand our relationship with God and build our confidence in His plan for us.

2. *Death is not the end*

Job poses the question: "If a man dies, shall he live again?" (Job 14:14). Because Jesus Christ paid the price for our sins, died for us, and was resurrected, we all will live again. Knowing that death is a part of God's plan and not the end of our existence gives us hope and increased purpose.

3. *Love God*

When in the most pain and when death seemed certain, Job boldly declared his love for God and that he would always love God. There are many ways we can show our love to God. Through serving others and obeying God's commandments, we not only show God we love Him but also help others feel God's love through us. In the end, Job was blessed immensely for his faithfulness and dedication to living a righteous life, a life that showed his love for God. We too will receive blessings from our loving Heavenly Father as we show our love to Him.

Source: https://www.mormon.org/blog/lifelessonsfromjob

TRUTHFULNESS: CHAPTER 4

Fourthly, to be positively influential in your Christian life and faith, you must be *truthful*. We need to be truthful to ourselves before we can be truthful to others. Being truthful can be used in the same context as having integrity. To have a clear understanding of this chapter and how it links to faith, I will first define truthfulness and integrity. According to the Oxford Dictionary:

a) *Truthfulness*: the fact of being realistic or true to life; realism.

b) *Integrity*: The quality of being honest and having strong moral principles.

From the above definitions we can conclude that truthfulness and integrity are interlinked by honesty. To be honest starts within ourselves before we try harder to be honest in front of other people. Truthfulness and integrity should not only be for approval by people but it should also be about the approval of God. 2 Timothy 2:15: "Do your best to present yourself to God as one approved, a worker who does not need to be ashamed and who correctly handles the word of truth."

The Bible is brutally honest in exposing the failures of some of the great men and women of faith when it comes to lying. Abraham, Sarah, Moses, Aaron, Isaac, Rebekah, Jacob, Rachel, and David all lied, along with Peter in the New Testament.

If these saints struggled with being truthful, then none of us is exempt. So we all need to take Paul's exhortation to heart.

Ephesians 4:25: "Therefore, laying aside falsehood, speak truth each one of you with his neighbour, for we are members of one another."

"Therefore" takes us back to the preceding context. Paul has told us generally how we are to be different from our former life of corruption "in accordance with the lusts of deceit". Since God has changed us through the gospel, we are to live in the light of the truth by putting off the old life, being renewed in the spirit of our minds and putting on the new life (Ephesians 4:22-24). It's easy to hear that and think, "Amen, preach, it Brother Paul." But we leave it out there in the realm of generalities and don't apply it specifically.

So beginning in Ephesians 4:25 (and going through Ephesians 6:9), Paul gets specific. He goes from preaching to meddling. He names a bunch of specific sins from our old life that we are to put off and godly behaviours that we are to put on. While there are some exceptions, his usual method is to state the sinful behaviour that we are to put off, the godly behaviour that we are to put on and the motive or reason for the positive behaviour.

In Ephesians 4:25 he is saying, we who have experienced the new birth must lay aside falsehood and speak the truth, because we are members of one another. To define our terms, truth is an accurate representation of the facts. Especially, truth is conformity to God's standards as revealed in His Word in

John 17:17. God is the truth and He always speaks the truth. Falsehood or lying is any deliberate misrepresentation of the facts.

Also, keep in mind the directive of Ephesians 4:15, that we must speak the truth in love. We must be kind and gracious when we speak the truth. We need to phrase the truth in a way that is least offensive and most sensitive to the other person's feelings. We need to apply the golden rule: how would I want someone else to tell me this truth? I must speak it in the same manner.

Also, being truthful does not mean that we need to reveal everything we know about a matter. God does not do that with us. If you need to keep a confidence or if you think that making the truth known would be damaging, you may simply reply, "I'm not free to talk about that matter".

Being truthful does not require sharing your thoughts on everything. If being silent would imply agreement when you disagree, you may need to clarify things. But sometimes wisdom requires keeping your thoughts to yourself (Proverbs 10:19).

Let's explore Paul's thought here:

1. *The new birth is the starting point for a life of truthfulness.* As I said, "therefore" takes us back to Ephesians 4:22, where Paul has just said that we are to "lay aside the old self, which is being corrupted in accordance with the lusts of deceit." Deceit permeated the old life.

We were deceived by sin and we deceived others by our self-serving hypocrisy and greed. It also takes us back to Ephesians 4:24, where Paul said that we are to "put on the new self, which in the likeness of God has been created in righteousness and holiness of the truth." Truth characterizes our new life in Christ.

We are to live in accordance with the truth which is in Jesus (Ephesians 4:21). And we are now to live as truthful people.

Some unbelievers are truthful people, but usually their truthfulness is self-serving. They take great pride that their word is good. Or, they are truthful because they fear the punishment or shame that comes if their duplicity comes to light. But only those who have received new life through God's grace can be truthful out of the motive of pleasing and glorifying Him.

2. Those who are new creatures in Christ must lay aside falsehood and speak the truth. Maybe you're thinking, "Great, but how do you do it?"

Five strategies for becoming a person of truth

> a) *Recognize The Source Of Truth And The Source Of Falsehood.*

God is the source of truth. He is the only true God, whose word is truth (John 17:3). As such, He cannot lie (Titus 1:2; Hebrews 6:18). Jesus Christ is the embodiment of the truth (John 14:6; Ephesians 4:21). He spoke the truth (John 8:45). The Holy Spirit is the Spirit of truth (John 14:17).

Satan is the source of falsehood and lies. Jesus called Satan "a liar and the father of lies" (John 8:44). Satan introduced "the lie" in the garden, when he implied that God was lying in the threat of punishment if Eve ate the forbidden fruit. He deceived Eve with the lie (Genesis 3:4), "You surely will not die" We need to keep in mind who is the source of truth and who is the source of falsehood because our culture strongly pressures us into compromising the truth. This is especially true with the postmodern philosophy that tells us that there is no such thing as absolute truth.

b) Recognize The Importance Of Truthfulness To God.

Truthfulness is important to God because He is the God of truth who hates lying and falsehood. Since falsehood is contrary to God's holy nature and is, in fact, a part of Satan's rebellious nature, God hates it.

In Proverbs 6:16-19, Solomon lists seven things that God hates. Two of the seven have to do with lying. Proverbs 12:22 states, "Lying lips are an abomination to the Lord, but those who deal faithfully are His delight."

Truthfulness is important to God because truth is the basis for all communication. The instant that Adam and Eve sinned, they experienced a breakdown in the close fellowship with God and with one another that they had known before the fall. They tried to hide from God and they were uncomfortable with their nakedness before one another.

When God confronted Adam, he blamed Eve for his sin and she blamed the serpent. We all have struggled with communication ever since. When you think about it, it's ridiculous not to be honest before God, because He knows our every thought. But we still try to hide our sins from Him.

At the heart of good communication and close relationships is trust.

If you do not trust someone, you instinctively draw back and protect yourself. If you think that he will take personal matters that you share in confidence and broadcast them to others, you will not open up and share your heart.

Distrust results in distance in relationships and dishonesty causes distrust. You can spend a lifetime building trust in your marriage or on the job, but one stupid lie can erode that trust in an instant. ***So, truthfulness is very important to God, because it is the basis for all communication***.

c)   Choose To Obey God By Making A Prior Commitment Not To Lie, But Rather To Speak The Truth.

First, you must choose to obey God. When Paul addresses this subject, he does not say, "Go to a therapist and try to figure out why you are prone to lying. There must be something in the way your parents treated you at the root of this problem" Nor does he say, "Pray for victory in this area". Rather, he says, "Stop lying and start speaking the truth" In other words, choose to obey God.

Second, make a prior commitment not to lie. In other words, you must decide not to lie before you get into a situation that hits you broadside. Paul says here that you must decisively throw off lying as you would throw off dirty, smelly clothes. It is part of the old life of corruption and deceit, so as a new creature in Christ, commit yourself to say no to the temptation to lie.

You have to make this commitment before the temptation hits because it's easy to get trapped into lying. Note how

Satan set up Peter for his fall. The servant girl who kept the door said to Peter (John 18:17): "You are not also one of this man's disciples, are you?" The question begs for a negative answer. Peter fell into sin by replying, "I am not."

Maybe your dad says, "You don't know how this scratch got onto the fender of the car, do you?" Be careful. It's so easy to say, "No, what scratch?" And then, once you've lied, it's even more difficult to correct yourself and tell the truth the next time. So, you dig yourself in deeper with another lie and another one, until it becomes a habit pattern of sin.

Third, make a prior commitment to tell the truth, even if it makes you look bad. Usually, we lie because the truth will expose our sin. Or, we fear what will happen if we're honest.

When Abraham went down to Egypt to escape the famine, he told Sarah to say that she was his sister, because he was afraid that, if the Egyptians knew that she was his wife, they would kill him in order to take her (Genesis 12:10-20). He justified the lie because it was half true.

She was the daughter of his father, but not of his mother. But, the truth was that she also was his wife. Not learning his lesson the first time, Abraham repeated the same lie years later with Abimelech (Genesis 20:1-18). Isaac later followed dad's steps with the same sin (Genesis 26:7-11). Each time, it was out of fear of what might happen if they told the truth. Such fear never stems from faith in God.

One way to begin this battle to become a person of truth is to resolve to speak the truth even in small matters. Invariably, those who fail in major ways, such as perjury, fraud or illegal cover-ups, don't begin there. They lie about small things, until their conscience is callused. Lying doesn't bother them anymore. Then, they get hit with a major temptation that could send them to prison. Out of habit and panic, they lie. It is far better to be scrupulously honest about everything.

So, to lay aside falsehood and speak the truth, recognize the source of truth and of falsehood. Recognize the importance of truth to God. Choose to obey God by making a prior commitment to speak the truth in every situation.

d) Confess Your Sins Immediately, First To God And Then To The Ones You Have Sinned Against.

We fall into a habit of lying because we don't want God or others to know about our sin. As I said, it's ridiculous to think that we can hide our falsehood from God. He sees the hidden thoughts of our hearts (Hebrews 4:13). But we mistakenly think that it is to our advantage to hide our sins from others. It is not, because invariably the truth comes out and our sin is exposed.

The more we have covered up, the more it erodes any sense of trust. It's far better to ask forgiveness, even after a minor falsehood, to keep your conscience tender and to maintain trust in relationships. Proverbs 28:13 says, "He who conceals his transgressions will not prosper, but he who confesses and forsakes them will find compassion."

e) Consider The Consequences Of Lying.

Proverbs 19:5 warns, "A false witness will not go unpunished, and he who tells lies will not escape" (see, also, Proverbs 19:9; 21:28).

Although you may be able to cite cases of those who have lied and gotten away with it, they didn't get away with it before God. If you sow falsehood, you won't reap God's blessing. Ask yourself the following questions about lying:

How could my lying bring glory to God?

Our chief end is to glorify God and enjoy Him forever. Everything we do should be for His glory (1 Corinthians 10:31). It is hard to conceive of how a lie could glorify the God of truth Who cannot lie.

How will my lying affect other believers?

We will consider this more in a moment. But, since lying erodes trust and leads to breakdowns in communication, lying is not for the good of others. You may think that it protects them, but invariably it hurts them.

How will my lying affect my family?

If your mate has reason to doubt your truthfulness, it will create distance between you. If your children see you bending the truth, they won't need to be taught to follow your example. Rather, they should see you telling the truth, even when it costs you. On the occasions when a clerk gives you too much change, use those occasions to teach your children the value of honesty.

How will my lying affect my testimony before unbelievers?

People read your life. They know that you profess to be a Christian and attend church. If they see you lying on the job, or keeping quiet about the truth when it is to your financial advantage, you have no basis for telling them about the Saviour. If a boss asks you to cover for him by lying, you need to be ready to graciously refuse and explain why. He may not like you and he may even fire you, but your testimony is worth much more than a job.

How will my lying affect my eternity?

I am not saying that you will lose your salvation by lying. As I said, some great men and women of faith were guilty of lying. But I am saying that if you claim to be a Christian, but you continue to live as you did before you became a Christian, you need to take a serious look at whether your faith in Christ is genuine.

Those who are characterized by lying or who always excuse it in some way are not giving any evidence that they have been created anew in righteousness and holiness of the truth. Revelation 21:8 warns with regard to all liars, "their part will be in the lake that burns with fire and brimstone, which is the second death". As Christians, we must fight our fleshly tendency towards lying. We must become people of truth. At the end of our verse, Paul tells us why.

3. The motive for laying aside falsehood and speaking the truth is that we are members of one another.

Paul already used the analogy of the body of Christ in connection with speaking the truth in love (Ephesians 4:14-16). Here, he brings it up again, citing Zechariah 8:16, where the Jews as the restored people of God are exhorted to speak truth with one another. But, Paul adds this reason, that we are members of one another.

The health of your physical body depends on truthful communication between the members through the nervous system. If you put your finger on a hot stove and your nerves do not relay to the brain, "this is hot", you will suffer severe injury. A person with leprosy lacks this communication between the nerves and the brain. He can actually destroy his own hand without knowing it.

This means that if you lie to your mate or to another member of the body of Christ, you are injuring yourself and, even worse, you are injuring Christ, because He is one with His body. So if you would not deliberately injure yourself, and if you don't want to injure your family and, most importantly, if you don't want to injure the Saviour who gave Himself for you on the cross, you must develop the habit of laying aside falsehood and speaking truth, for we are members of one another.

Source: https://bible.org/seriespage/lesson-32-tell-truth-ephesians-425

Ananias and Sapphira

Acts 5:1-11 NIV:

Now a man named Ananias, together with his wife Sapphira, also sold a piece of property. With his wife's full knowledge he kept back part of the money for himself, but brought the rest and put it at the apostles' feet.

Then Peter said, "Ananias, how is it that Satan has so filled your heart that you have lied to the Holy Spirit and have kept for yourself some of the money you received for the land? Didn't it belong to you before it was sold? And after it was sold, wasn't the money at your disposal? What made you think of doing such a thing? You have not lied just to human beings but to God."

When Ananias heard this, he fell down and died. And great fear seized all who heard what had happened. Then some young men came forward, wrapped up his body, and carried him out and buried him. About three hours later his wife came in, not knowing what had happened. Peter asked her, "Tell me, is this the price you and Ananias got for the land?" "Yes," she said, "that is the price."

Peter said to her, "How could you conspire to test the Spirit of the Lord? Listen. The feet of the men who buried your husband are at the door, and they will carry you out also."

At that moment she fell down at his feet and died. Then the young men came in and, finding her dead, carried her out and buried her beside her husband. Great fear seized the whole church and all who heard about these events.

In Conclusion

The truth is that we are all guilty of lying directly or indirectly, just like Ananias and Sapphira, but the most important thing is repentance by seeking for forgiveness from the people involved and from God. I remember a funny short story. We visited our relatives in Mafutseni on the 25th of December 2018.

We took a wrong turn and we got lost but later we found the right route and we arrived safely. When we got there we didn't mention about getting lost because we didn't want to be humiliated, so we lied. We said that we got delayed along the way.

We got away with it because we didn't harm anyone by lying but the truth remains that we were untruthful. We felt the guilt, but we didn't do anything about it. 1 John 1:8: "If we say that we have no sin, we are deceiving ourselves and the truth is not in us."

A lie is a lie no matter how small it seems, so it is important to guide our tongue always. For example, some students in schools or universities copy or steal exam papers and they get away with it, but the guilt will never go away unless they confess and repent.

Repentance

Acts 3:18-19: **18** "But this is how God fulfilled what he had foretold through all the prophets, saying that his Messiah would suffer. **19** Repent, then, and turn to God, so that your sins may be wiped out, that times of refreshing may come from the Lord."

In these two verses we can see that the solution to lying or not being truthful is *repentance*. Repentance simply means "turn" or "return". Two requisites of repentance included are "to turn from evil, and to turn to the good". Most critical theologically is the idea of returning to God, or turning away from evil.

If one turns away from God, apostasy is indicated. Three times Ezekiel included God's call to the people of Israel: "Repent. Turn from your idols and renounce all your detestable practices." "Repent. Turn away from all your offenses", "Turn. Turn from your evil ways". Such a call was characteristic of the prophets.

Confession of sins is both commanded and frequently illustrated. When one is guilty of various sins, "he must confess in what way he has sinned" in order to receive atonement and forgiveness. Thus, confession belongs to repentance, and is needed for divine forgiveness. A great prophecy or promise is given in the Book of Isaiah: "The Redeemer will come to Zion, to those in Jacob who repent of their sins".

In the New Testament, the key term for repentance is metanoia - It has two usual senses: a "change of mind" and "regret/remorse". In both books of Mark and Matthew, Jesus began His public proclamation with the call "Repent".

In addition, Paul is said to have preached to both Jews and Gentiles/Greeks to "turn to God in repentance and have faith in our Lord Jesus".

Repentance is only a condition of salvation and not its meritorious ground. The motives for repentance are chiefly found in the goodness of God, in divine love, in the pleading desire to have sinners saved, in the inevitable consequences of sin, in the universal demands of the gospel, and in the hope of spiritual life and membership in the kingdom of heaven. Source: https://www.biblestudytools.com/topical-verses/repentance-bible-verses/

Characteristics of Repentance

Matthew 4:17; Revelation 3:19

God is our standard, not others. We must look to God in order to correctly see our sin. Repentance is that mighty change in mind, heart, and life wrought by the Spirit of God. (Richard Trench)

- *True Repentance Means Change.* You can't repent and remain the same. Ezekiel 8:18: "Therefore I also will act in fury. My eye will not spare nor will I have pity; and though they cry in My ears with a loud voice, I will not hear them."

  Why do our prayers seem powerless?

  Isaiah 1:15: "When you spread out your hands, I will hide My eyes from you; Even though you make many prayers, I will not hear. Your hands are full of blood."

  Hebrews 4:16: "Let us therefore come boldly to the throne of grace that we may obtain mercy and find grace to help in time of need."

- *A change of mind*: "Metaknowa" a total change of mind.

  Psalm 51:3: "For I acknowledge my transgressions, and my sin *is* always before me."

  To "confess" means to agree with God about my sin; to no longer make rationalizations about my sin, no more excuses about why I sin.

- *A change of emotions*

  2 Corinthians 7:10: "For godly sorrow produces repentance *leading* to salvation, not to be regretted; but the sorrow of the world produces death."

  The "sorrow of the world" is sorrow for the consequences our sins produce.

  Godly sorrow is when we realize our sin breaks God's heart and then it breaks our heart. We must mourn over our sin and experience brokenness.

  Isaiah 53:5 "But He *was* wounded for our transgressions, *He was* bruised for our iniquities; the chastisement for our peace *was* upon Him, and by His stripes we are healed."

  Any time there is flippancy about sin; repentance hasn't taken place in our lives.

Psalm 51:17: "The sacrifices of God *are* a broken spirit, A broken and a contrite heart - These, O God, You will not despise."

- *A change in direction*

If you keep going back to the sin, then you have not truly been broken over your sin and have not really repented. You will have a new desire take place when you truly repent. You will have a hunger in your heart to walk with the Father.

- *True Repentance is Granted by God*
- *Repentance requires radical action*

True repentance is not generated by the flesh; it is granted by God.

2 Timothy 2:25: "in humility correcting those who are in opposition, if God perhaps will grant them repentance, so that they may know the truth".

Acts 11:18: "When they heard these things they became silent; and they glorified God, saying, Then God has also granted to the Gentiles repentance to life'."

Anytime our love for the Lord grows cold a change is needed.

- *God commands us to repent:* Acts 17:30: "Truly, these times of ignorance God overlooked, but now commands all men everywhere to repent".

2 Peter 3:9: "The Lord is not slack
concerning *His* promise, as some count slackness, but is
longsuffering toward us, not willing that any should
perish but that all should come to repentance."

- *True Repentance Is Often Missed*
- *Some repent in outward actions and not in the heart.*

Our love of sin remains.

Psalm 51:16-17: "For You do not desire sacrifice, or else
I would give *it;* You do not delight in burnt offering. 17
The sacrifices of God *are* a broken spirit, A broken and a
contrite heart - These, O God, You will not despise."

Joel 2:13: "So rend your heart, and not your garments;
Return to the LORD your God, For He *is* gracious and
merciful, slow to anger, and of great kindness; And He
relents from doing harm."

Our heart must be broken over our sin.

- *Some repent for fear of consequences instead of hatred
of sin.*

Ezekiel 36:31: "Then you will remember your evil ways
and your deeds that *were* not good; and you will loathe
yourselves in your own sight, for your iniquities and
your abominations."

- *Some repent to please others instead of God*

Psalm 51:4: "Against You, You only, have I sinned, and done *this* evil in Your sight - That You may be found just when You speak, *And* blameless when You judge."

Some repent so generally that it is not real repentance - Real repentance is real specific.

- *Some repent of some things but not others.*

  Psalm 119:128 "Therefore
  all *Your* precepts *concerning* all *things* I consider *to be* right; I hate every false way."

  Revelation 3:19 "As many as I love, I rebuke and chasten. Therefore be zealous and repent."

  "Zealous" means to desire eagerly.

- *True Repentance Is A Way Of Life*

  I need to be alert to anything that is in my life that causes me to go away form God.

  I need to learn to recognize sin when it comes.

- *True Repentance is Both Private and Corporate*

  Private/personal sin should be repented of privately.

  Corporate sin involves the church universal and local: divorce, apathy, complacency, lack of love for the lost, immodest dress, not seeking straying sheep, not having the anointing of God on lessons and sermon, worldly habits and actions.

- *True Repentance Is Both Vertical and Horizontal*

  Vertical – all sin is an affront to God.

  Psalm 51:4: "Against You, You only, have I sinned, and done *this* evil in Your sight -- That You may be found just when You speak, *And* blameless when You judge."

  Horizontal – when our sin has wronged others we must ask for their forgiveness

  Rule of confession: confession only goes as far as the effects and knowledge of your sin.

- *True Repentance Results in Joy*

  Psalm 85:6: "Will You not revive us again, That Your people may rejoice in You?"

  Nehemiah 8:17: "So the whole assembly of those who had returned from the captivity made booths and sat under the booths; for since the days of Joshua the son of Nun until that day the children of Israel had not done so. And there was very great gladness."

  Source: https://sermons.faithlife.com/sermons/70446-sf987-seven-characteristics-of-true-repentance-(matthew-4-17)

HAPPINESS: CHAPTER 5

Lastly, to be positively influential in your Christian life and faith, you must be *joyful*. Just imagine a pastor who is facing some difficult challenges coming to preach with a sad face. Do you think the congregation will believe in this pastor's faith? Certainly not. Adversities or trials should not determine our *happiness* in our faith. 1 Peter 4:13: "But rejoice in as much as you participate in the sufferings of Christ, so that you may be overjoyed when His glory is revealed".

When we think of happiness, we might feel that it is something that is so hard to capture. Joy is the deep and abiding presence of contentment, peace and pleasure. We can find our true happiness and joy within Jesus.

The Bible is filled with stories of Bible characters who found and chose happiness through God. Whether it is after unexpected blessings or through sharing His Good News, these stories focus on how God will always be there for His children. These bible stories will inspire you to become a happier person, by knowing that with God you can do anything. His timing is always right, as long as we trust in Him and follow His word.

Sarah Gets Unexpected Blessings

Sarah has long prayed to God to have a child with her husband, Abraham. While she begged Him to let her bear a son, she went years without being able to conceive. Sarah began to move on from her desire to have children and thought it would never happen.

One day, however, the Lord visited Sarah as He said He would and blessed her with her child, Isaac. Sarah was able to finally find *joy* in the unexpected and long-awaited blessings of her son.

While she of course felt *happy* after receiving her child, the real joy came in Sarah's recognition that God's timing was best. While life almost always never turns out in the way we expect it to, we have to be on the lookout for God's timing and His many hidden blessings. God brought Sarah the blessing of her son when she least expected it. God will do so for us, as well.

Jesus' Birth

Jesus' birth is a key story in the Bible because ***Jesus is the true source of our happiness***. The wise men only knew so much about who Jesus was and why He came to earth, but yet the Bible says that they were overcome with *joy*. Matthew 2:10: "When they saw the star, they rejoiced exceedingly with great joy. And going into the house they saw the child with Mary his mother and they fell down and worshiped him".

Knowing all we know today, we should also find extreme happiness in the story of Jesus' birth. Jesus is God's greatest gift to this earth. Because of Him, we have the hope of heaven and the promise of peace as we go through life.

Paul and Barnabas Share the Good News

We can obtain *joy* by spreading the Good News of Jesus' love, like Paul and Barnabas did in the bible. Paul and Barnabas were asked by God to spread the good news of Jesus' love. They

Reasons Why Every Believer in Jesus Christ Should Be Happy Always

Rejoice in the Lord always; again I will say, rejoice (Philippians 4:4). There is no way we can begin to number the blessings God has heaped upon those who believe in His Son, but here are a few spiritual blessings we should regularly recall, thank God for, and rejoice in:

1. We have eternal life and can never lose it;
2. We are one with Christ;
3. Jesus has paid for every sin we ever have and ever will commit;
4. God Himself is our Father;
5. There is absolutely no condemnation for us in Christ;
6. We are no longer slaves of sin or under its dominion;
7. We are joint heirs with Christ and will share in His reward;
8. We have a sympathetic high priest who intercedes for us night and day;
9. The Holy Spirit of God dwells in, empowers, comforts and counsels us;
10. Our God is our refuge, strength, and strong tower;
11. We have unlimited access to the throne of grace;
12. Nothing will ever separate us from God's love;
13. God is working all things for our good;
14. Someday we will be reunited with our loved ones who believed in Jesus;
15. The Creator of the universe hears our every prayer;
16. God has a purpose for our lives which He will certainly

fulfil;

17. God has prepared good works for us to walk in;

18. The angel of the Lord encamps around us 24/7;

19. God is in control of every detail of our lives;

20. Jesus will never leave us nor forsake us;

21. Every bit of pain we endure produces an eternal weight of glory beyond all comparison;

22. The One who watches over us neither slumbers nor sleeps;

23. God will make each one of His children into the likeness of His Son;

24. God will reward us for every good deed we do, no matter how small;

25. God will supply our every need;

26. Someday, Jesus will personally wipe away our every tear;

27. And someday we will gaze upon the glorious face of our Saviour for eternity.

Source: https://www.biblestudytools.com/blogs/mark-altrogge/27-reasons-why-every-believer-in-jesus-should-rejoice-always.html

Can Money Buy Happiness?

Five things we should know about money:

1. The More We Have, the More We Want

Ecclesiastes 5:10: He who loves silver will not be satisfied with silver; nor he who loves abundance, with increase. This also is vanity. Look up the richest tycoons in town. Meet them at the country club for a game of golf or tennis; discuss their dreams.

I predict you'll discover that they are focused on getting more, especially as more can be equated with their happiness.

You can be the poorest peasant or the richest land baron, yet it seems you'll always want more. The more we get, the more we want, the farther our happiness gets away from us. The fire is fed but never quenched.

Luke 12:15: Jesus said, "Take heed and beware of covetousness, for one's life does not consist in the abundance of the things he possesses".

There aren't many "Uncle Bud" Robinsons among us. Robinson, a well-known holiness preacher of an earlier generation, was taken by friends to New York and shown all the sights of the city. That night in his prayers, he said, "Lord, I thank You for letting me see all the sights of New York. And I thank You most of all that I didn't see a thing that I wanted."

Wouldn't it be wonderful to be truly content? To be eased of the burden for more accumulation, and to be at peace with where we are in life? *Why do we make ourselves miserable over what has no track record of satisfying?*

Part of Paul's incredible power in his ministry came from this trait, expressed in Philippians 4:11-12: "I have learned, in whatever state I am, to be content: I know how to be abased, and I know how to abound. Everywhere and in all things I have learned both to be full and to be hungry, both to abound and to suffer need". There is wisdom and power in knowing how to be content with much or little.

2. The More We Have, the More We Spend

Ecclesiastes 5:11: When goods increase, they increase who eat them; so what profit have the owners except to see them with their eyes?

The big promotion comes through with its expected raise. We could simply keep the same lifestyle and use the extra money wisely, but in a microsecond we are salivating over the prospect of new cars, new furniture, perhaps a second home. Solomon says that when possessions get thick, so do we. He wants to know, what's the point of having more money? We'll just go out and spend whatever we get. After all, a few more possessions never hurt anyone, especially if they supplied just a few moments of happiness, right?

The Message puts the concept this way: "The more loot you get, the more looters show up."

Author William MacDonald says, *"When a man's possessions increase, it seems there's a corresponding increase in the number of parasites who live off him: management consultants, tax advisers, accountants, lawyers, household employees, and sponging relatives."*

The more you have, the more you want. The more you want, the more you spend. The more you spend, the more you need. The more you need, the more you have to have.

3. The More We Have, the More We Worry

Ecclesiastes 5:12: The sleep of a labouring man is sweet, whether he eats little or much; but the abundance of the rich will not permit him to sleep.

When you can fit all your life's valuables in the backseat of your car, you can sleep well at night because you've cut down your "worry field".

By God's grace I can say I've never lost a night's sleep over the status of my investments.

Many people think that the more money they have, the happier they'll be, and the more soundly they'll sleep at night, but the opposite is true. The more they get, the more they worry about preserving it.

When money is your shield and bulwark, you'll spend all your time worrying about what will happen if you lose your shield. Thankfully, my Shield and Protector is One who has already said, "I will never leave you nor forsake you" (Hebrews 13:5).

When he was fifty-three years old, John D. Rockefeller was the world's only billionaire. His income was $1 million per week. But he was a sick man who lived on crackers and milk and could not sleep because he worried so much about his money. Eventually, he learned how to give money away and his health improved radically. As a philanthropist, he lived to celebrate his 98th birthday.

Lack of money flushes us out of self-satisfied isolation. It forces us to go out and meet people and to need some of them. *As we grow richer, we draw away from community.*

We miss a lot of the little graces and relational encounters that make life real and satisfying, that help bring a taste of true happiness—and we replace them with trinkets that never live up to their shiny allure.

4. The More We Have, the More We Lose

Ecclesiastes 5:13-14: *There is a severe evil which I have seen under the sun: riches kept for their owner to his hurt. But those riches perish through misfortune.* Let me be clear on this point, because it's easy to misunderstand what Solomon is saying. The essence of his message is this: You can't lose what you don't have.

We shouldn't avoid seeking things just because we could lose them. But we should realize from the very beginning that we are adding one more element to our lives, one more dependency, and one more responsibility. Anyone who has ever bought a home for the first time understands that concept.

We become attached to our possessions at our own risk because we now have so much more to lose. And soon our happiness, our joy, our peace depends on how protective we are of our possessions.

5. The More We Have, the More We Leave Behind

Ecclesiastes 5:14-17: *When he begets a son, there is nothing in his hand. As he came from his mother's womb, naked shall he return, to go as he came; and he shall take nothing from his labour which he may carry away in his hand. And this also is a severe evil—just exactly as he came, so shall he go. And what profit has he who has laboured for the wind? All his days he also eats in darkness, and he has much sorrow and sickness and anger.*

We all know the modern translation of this one: *You can't take it with you when you die.*

It's just common sense. You pay sweat and toil for the things you accumulate. But you never own anything permanently; you only rent it for a season, until you pass from this earth.

Your precious possessions, even if they outlast you, will belong to someone else.

The flip side of that coin is positive: Much good has been done by sizeable bequests to charities, Christian ministries, or individuals. *Accumulation can work hand in hand with goals for God's kingdom. For now, we only need to remember that in eternal terms, there is no own—only loan.* And the more we give away, the less we worry, and the more happiness we can find here.

Jesus reminds us to act wisely, therefore, and invest in the treasures that are indeed permanent, for they are fixed in heaven. (Matthew 6:20-21*): "But lay up for yourselves treasures in* *heaven, where neither moth nor rust destroys and where thieves do not break in and steal. For where your treasure is, there your heart will be also".*

Source: https://www.davidjeremiah.org/happiness/can-money-buy-happiness

As we may recall at the beginning of this book, I mentioned a point about the devil but we didn't discuss it further. The point was: The devil disguises himself as a sheep in a wolf skin (be vigilant). 2 Corinthians 11: 14 CEV: "And it is no wonder. Even Satan tries to make himself look like an angel of light."

Do not let the Devil Steal your Happiness: Why is it important to maintain our joy?

The Bible tells us in 1 Peter 5:8 NIV: "Be alert and of sober mind. Your enemy the devil prowls around like a roaring lion looking for someone to devour. John 10:10a, NIV: The thief comes only to steal and kill and destroy.

The enemy wants to keep you trapped in a place of frustration, unhappiness, sorrow, heartbreak or one of many other devices. The Word of God tells us that it's God Who gives us life and life more abundantly. John 10:10b, NIV: "I have come that they may have life, and have it to the fullest".

We live in tough times with tough circumstances. The key to maintaining our joy is recognizing that God is bigger than any problem that we have.

Why joy? I don't think we understand the power of joy nor have the right tools to make sure joy is part of our lives. There is a place that God has that is far better for us.

I'm not talking about just happiness either. Happiness is only an emotion and is temporary. What God offers is more powerful than that – true joy.

Nehemiah 8:10b NIV: "The joy of the LORD is your strength." This means you are given strength to overcome when you have true joy.

Proverbs 17:22a NIV: "A cheerful heart is good medicine." When you have joy it's like you have taken a dose of medicine to help your body feel better.

Joy is a condition of your heart

The condition of your heart is significant because it is from where everything flows. *When your heart is right then your life becomes full and fruitful.* So, when you place joy inside the depths of your heart, you become strong enough to fight. You become unworried, untroubled, at ease, peaceful, fulfilled and content, especially during the worst of circumstances.

How do you maintain your joy?

- Meditate on the scriptures, particularly about joy, peace and contentment
- Pray
- Rejoice

Philippians 4:4 NIV: "Rejoice in the Lord always. I will say it again: Rejoice." Rejoicing when things are going well is easy. It's in the midst of a trial that it becomes challenging. It might not be easy the first time but God wants you to rejoice and keep rejoicing. Regardless of our circumstances, however dark they might be, we're not abandoned, and we're not destroyed.

There's an incomparable power within each one of us that can't be shaken when we're grounded in Christ. Certainly, we'll have days that bring us down to our knees in tears, but the same power that raised Christ from the dead gives us the strength and the hope to get back on our feet. 2 Corinthians 4:18 NIV: "For the things which are seen are temporal; but the things which are not seen are eternal."

Bring your problems to God

Philippians 4:6-8 NIV: "Do not be anxious about anything, but in every situation, by prayer and petition, with thanksgiving, present your requests to God. And the peace of God, which transcends all understanding, will guard your hearts and your minds in Christ Jesus.

Finally, brothers and sisters, whatever is true, whatever is noble, whatever is right, whatever is pure, whatever is lovely, whatever is admirable—if anything is excellent or praiseworthy—think about such things." God wants you to bring your troubles to Him through prayer He wants you to praise Him through the storms. He does not want you to walk around sorrowful, downhearted, gloomy, unhappy or heartbroken. God wants you to be filled with an inexpressible and glorious joy.

desires. Never let success blind you but always be content with whatever you have and don't forget to be generous because there is no guarantee that what you have today you will still have tomorrow.

The Bible is brutally honest in exposing the failures of some of the great men and women of faith when it comes to lying. Abraham, Sarah, Moses, Aaron, Isaac, Rebekah, Jacob, Rachel, and David all lied, along with Peter in the New Testament. If these saints struggled with being truthful, then none of us is exempt. So we all need to take Paul's exhortation to heart. Ephesians 4:25: "Therefore, laying aside falsehood, speak *truth* each one of you with his neighbour, for we are members of one another."

Lack of money flushes us out of self-satisfied isolation. It forces us to go out and meet people and to need some of them. *As we grow richer, we draw away from community.* We miss a lot of the little graces and relational encounters that make life real and satisfying, that help bring a taste of true *happiness*—and we replace them with trinkets that never live up to their shiny allure.

References

1. https://m.imdb.com/title/tt0113483/plotsummary. Accessed on 31 December 2018

2. https://www.gotquestions.org/Nebuchadnezzars-dream.html. Accessed on 1 January 2019

3. https://www.gotquestions.org/fruitful-Christian.html. Accessed on 2 January 2019

4. https://www.theodysseyonline.com/sharing-our-testimony. Accessed on 3 January 2019

5. https://biblereasons.com/testimony/. Accessed on 4 January 2019

6. https://en.m.wikipedia.org/wiki/The_Italian_Job_(2003_film). Accessed on 5 January 2019

7. https://www.biblestudytools.com/topical-verses/faith-bible-verses/. Accessed on 5 January 2019

8. Devotional by John Piper: https://www.desiringgod.org/articles/five-purposes-for-suffering. Accessed on 5 January 2019

9. By Jack Wellman: https://www.whatchristianswanttoknow.com/job-bible-story-summary-with-lesson/. Accessed on 6 January 2019

10. https://www.gotquestions.org/life-Job.html. Accessed on 7 January 2019

11. https://www.mormon.org/blog/lifelessonsfromjob. Access on 7 January 2019

12. By Steven J. Cole: https://bible.org/seriespage/lesson-32-tell-truth-ephesians-425. Accessed on 8 January 2019

13. https://www.biblestudytools.com/topical-verses/repentance-bible-verses/. Accessed on 8 January 2019

14. By Timothy McGhee: https://sermons.faithlife.com/sermons/70446-sf987-seven-characteristics-of-true-repentance-(matthew-4-17). Accessed on 9 January 2019

15. By Megan Bailey: https://www.beliefnet.com/inspiration/galleries/bible-stories-that-inspire-us-to-be-happier-people.aspx. Accessed on 10 January 2019

16. By Mark Altrogge: https://www.biblestudytools.com/blogs/mark-altrogge/27-reasons-why-every-believer-in-jesus-should-rejoice-always.html. Accessed on 10 January 2019

17. By Dr. David Jeremiah: https://www.davidjeremiah.org/happiness/can-money-buy-happiness. Accessed on 10 January 2019

18. By Kathy Davis: http://navarre.church/blog-home/2016/8/16/dont-let-the-devil-steal-your-joy. Accessed on 10 January 2019

19. Bishop Tshalo Katsunga's teachings in Gospel Ramah Church: http://www.ramah.org.za/, Cape Town, South Africa. From 15 January 2013 – 31 December 2017

20. Fr. Martin McCormack's influential quotes on Facebook and his positive attitude and influence in general: https://web.facebook.com/martin.mccormack.7946

21. Bishop Absalom Mnisi for his great teachings and amazing understanding of the Word of God